MW01092678

"Trauma, exhaustion, shame, and pain are all part of life. However, the brighter side of life consists of love, contentment, peace, and joy. The latter are spiritual fruit that develop throughout the course of life. In the book *Sacred Attachment*, Michael John Cusick understands that both sides of the coin are part of the divine plan. . . . He takes the reader on a spiritual journey from growing up with fear and anxiety about his faith to becoming an adult who delights in the blessed assurance of experiencing a more intimate relationship with Yahweh. And that is why we were created!"

**Barbara L. Peacock,** founder of Peacock Soul Care and author of *Soul Care in African American Practice*

"I absolutely love this book! Cusick not only brilliantly unpacks insights from Scripture and psychology, but with breathtaking courage and generosity, he reveals his life to us so we can experience the joy of wholeness."

**Ken Shigematsu,** pastor of Tenth Church in Vancouver, British Columbia, and author of *Now I Become Myself: How Deep Grace Heals Our Shame and Restores Our True Self*

"Some of us are tempted to believe that our struggles or sufferings push God away. In fact, the grace, mercy, and love of God are drawn to that which is wounded, wayward, or broken in us. Michael Cusick's stories, from both his life and his walking alongside others, powerfully display the surprising and even scandalous grace of our God. I felt encouraged and understood as I read this book. I highly recommend it."

**Alan Fadling,** cofounder of Unhurried Living Inc. and author of *A Non-Anxious Life*

"We don't believe we are loved until we feel it in our chests. Given how infrequently this happens, no wonder we are as exhausted as we are. But thanks be to God, . . . Michael Cusick takes us on a deeply personal and comprehensively practical journey that invites the reader into the wide place to stand of which the psalmist writes. A wide place in which you become the beauty and goodness that you have been destined to become. Read this book and rest. Read this book and be revealed. But mostly read this book and know—in your chest—what it means to be loved."

**Curt Thompson,** author of *The Soul of Shame* and *The Deepest Place: Suffering and the Formation of Hope*

"With compassion and vulnerability, *Sacred Attachment* invites us to address the gap between who we are and who God created us to be. Michael Cusick has written a gentle yet powerful book drawn from a blend of biblical insight, psychological acumen, and ancient Christian wisdom that is deeply needed in our world today. This compelling resource is an absolute gift."

**Aundi Kolber,** therapist and author of *Try Softer* and *Strong like Water*

"As a personal witness and beneficiary of Michael Cusick's trauma-informed spiritual care, I can attest to the sacred wisdom offered in these pages. Among the treasures you'll find herein, you'll find the truth of how it is that the divine life can be known and experienced directly through our wounds and in our shadows. This revelation is perhaps the primary medicine and mercy that God dispenses through Michael to those in need of healing, whether in his clinic and intensive retreats or through his books. I'm forever grateful."

**Bradley Jersak**, principal at St. Stephen's University and author of *A More Christlike God*

"As someone who makes a living writing at the intersection of faith and culture, I'm inundated with stories of people who are spirituality disillusioned. Too many have been told their doubts and objections, brokenness and struggles, orientations and identities are incompatible with living in the arms of divine love. Michael John Cusick offers us something we need more than we know: a trauma-informed spirituality of compassion. *Sacred Attachment* presents a path for life with God that is wide-armed and clear-eyed. This remarkable book makes the good news feel, well, good. And it has come to us not a moment too soon."

**Jonathan Merritt**, award-winning columnist and author of *Learning to Speak God from Scratch*

"With disarming vulnerability, Michael John Cusick masterfully weaves his own dramatic story of healing with clinical insights he's gleaned in over thirty years of working as a therapist and spiritual director. Along the way he exposes and names our own spiritual wounds while guiding us to rest in divine love—the one true place where we are seen, soothed, safe, and secure. If you are sick and tired of trying to acquire or attain God's affection, or trying to muster up faith, this book is a must read."

**Ian Morgan Cron**, author of *The Fix* and *The Road Back to You*

"With *Sacred Attachment*, Michael John Cusick paints a beautiful, multifaceted picture of healing that inspires the imagination and invites deep personal reflection. I couldn't put it down. Cusick's willingness to share his own journey through pain adds depth and nuance to his expertise as a clinician. This book is a moving testament to the power of grace and restoration. It will not only nourish your soul, it will help you heal."

**Alison Cook**, podcast host and author of *I Shouldn't Feel This Way* and *Boundaries For Your Soul*

"This book delivers the full experience of restoring the soul. Following Michael John Cusick's approach to trauma-informed, clinical soul-care, this book offers wisdom for healing and restoration. The brilliance of the message comes from its trustworthy source, Michael's own life and experiences. His gifted and authentic teaching invites the reader to open up their inner world and be transformed by the sacred truth that love has you."

**Kyle J Wisdom**, deputy director at the International Institute for Religious Freedom

"Michael Cusick's story is so compelling, not least because it's in and through it that the very good and very beautiful story of the safe, secure, seeing, and soothing love of God can be revealed. For all who feel too broken, this is an invitation to the deep and sacred work of healing that is possible."

**Chuck DeGroat**, professor of pastoral care and Christian spirituality at Western Theological Seminary and author of *When Narcissism Comes to Church*

"I cannot express how deeply this book resonated with me. It feels like a deep confirmation of who I am and the identity I am meant to embrace in the world. Cusick's insights are not just thought-provoking; they serve as a powerful affirmation of truth and discovery. The life experiences that Michael John Cusick shares throughout the pages of this book have led him to a level of expertise that is both inspiring and transformative. His wisdom is profound and has the potential to liberate thousands from the uncertainties and struggles of real life. I truly believe that the insights found within this book are incredibly valuable and can spark change in the lives of many."

**Tyler Johnson**, cofounder of Surge Network, Missional Training Center, and Arizona 1:27

"Michael John Cusick is beautifully honest and compelling. He invites us to explore God's wild attachment and our audacious response. It's a read that will awaken the parts that have grown numb."

**Christy Bauman**, author of *Her Rites*

"I love this book. I love it for many reasons: the writing is excellent, funny, and vulnerable. But what I love most about this book is what it did to me as I read it. It gently exposed my deep longings to be seen, safe, soothed, and secure, while dismantling my false narratives about how to achieve them. It moved me toward a new paradigm for a new kind of faith, one in which my soul had been longing for. By the time I was done reading it, I was convinced as never before that love truly has me, and I am now unafraid to invite God into the gaps in my life. This book soars, each chapter better than the last. No matter what you do this year, read this book."

**James Bryan Smith**, author of *The Good and Beautiful God*

# SACRED
# ATTACHMENT

### ESCAPING SPIRITUAL
### EXHAUSTION *AND*
### TRUSTING *IN* DIVINE LOVE

MICHAEL JOHN CUSICK

An imprint of InterVarsity Press
Downers Grove, Illinois

**InterVarsity Press**
P.O. Box 1400 | Downers Grove, IL 60515-1426
ivpress.com | email@ivpress.com

©2025 by Michael John Cusick

InterVarsity Press® is the publishing division of InterVarsity Christian Fellowship/USA®. For more information, visit intervarsity.org.

All Scripture quotations, unless otherwise indicated, are taken from The Holy Bible, New International Version®, NIV®. Copyright © 1973, 1978, 1984, 2011 by Biblica, Inc.™ Used by permission of Zondervan. All rights reserved worldwide. www.zondervan.com. "NIV" and "New International Version" are trademarks registered in the United States Patent and Trademark Office by Biblica, Inc.™

Scripture quotations marked MSG are taken from The Message, copyright © 1993, 2002, 2018 by Eugene H. Peterson. Used by permission of NavPress. All rights reserved. Represented by Tyndale House Publishers.

While any stories in this book are true, some names and identifying information may have been changed to protect the privacy of individuals.

Published in association with Helmers Literary Services.

The publisher cannot verify the accuracy or functionality of website URLs used in this book beyond the date of publication.

Cover design: David Fassett
Interior design: Daniel van Loon
Images: Moment via Getty Images: © SEAN GLADWELL, © kampee patisena

ISBN 978-1-5140-0831-7 (print) | ISBN 978-1-5140-0832-4 (digital)

Printed in the United States of America ∞

**Library of Congress Cataloging-in-Publication Data**
Names: Cusick, Michael John, 1964- author.
Title: Sacred attachment : escaping spiritual exhaustion and trusting in
   divine love / Michael John Cusick.
Description: Downers Grove, IL : IVP Formatio, [2025] | Includes
   bibliographical references.
Identifiers: LCCN 2024025655 (print) | LCCN 2024025656 (ebook) | ISBN
   9781514008317 (print) | ISBN 9781514008324 (digital)
Subjects: LCSH: Cusick, Michael John, 1964- | Christian biography–United
   States. | BISAC: RELIGION / Christian Living / Spiritual Growth |
   RELIGION / Christian Ministry / Counseling & Recovery
Classification: LCC BR1725.C849 A3 2025  (print) | LCC BR1725.C849  (ebook)
   | DDC 277.308/2–dc23/eng/20240807
LC record available at https://lccn.loc.gov/2024025655
LC ebook record available at https://lccn.loc.gov/2024025656

31  30  29  28  27  26  25  |  13  12  11  10  9  8  7  6  5  4  3  2  1

*For Jewels—the love of my life.*

*There are two kinds of Christians: list makers and storytellers. Answering one question reveals the difference, "What does it take to be a Christian?"*

*List makers will talk about doctrines you must believe or commandments you must keep. As long as you believe the right things or do the right things, that's what makes you a Christian.*

*Storytellers, on the other hand, will say: "Let me tell you about my grandmother . . ." That's when I lean in, because I find the art of Christian living far more compelling than a theological argument.*

*It didn't used to be that way, though. When I was a young man, I relished the opportunity to jump into the middle of doctrinal scrums over Christian beliefs. But these days, I'd rather hear about an embodied faith—a story that must be imagined to be believed.*

RODNEY REEVES

# CONTENTS

# 1

# SPINNING

## ESCAPING AND EXPERIENCING
## GOD'S EMBRACE

*There are parts of life that can't be gotten out of, and I have had
to learn, here, that we are all, at the end, held somehow.*

TA-NEHISI COATES

A bitter cold Sunday morning and the seven Cusicks, including my
four-year-old self, are crammed into our maroon Pontiac station
wagon for the long ride to Carmel of the Holy Family, a Roman
Catholic convent. My father's sister is a cloistered Carmelite nun.
In the unspoken pecking order of Catholic religious vocations, life
as a Carmelite is the military equivalent of becoming a Navy SEAL.
Not for the faint of heart.

The Carmelites go all the way back to the fourteen hundreds.
Like Saint Teresa of Ávila, Saint Thérèse of Lisieux, and Saint John
of the Cross, they make vows of chastity, poverty, and obedience
while choosing to withdraw from the world into a community devoted to contemplating the love and mystery of Christ.

Family visits to Carmel felt like Christmas morning—and Hal-
loween, wrapped together and placed under the tree. There were
smiles and laughter. But it also felt a little spooky because once
inside the convent the nuns were restricted to greeting visitors from

behind the grille–a metal grid of bars preventing the nuns from having physical contact with the outside world. So when you're four years old, no matter how much your parents explain about monastic vows and devotion to God, and you visit your aunt and a group of nuns behind bars, it still seems like you're visiting a prison full of women dressed like penguins.

After the initial excitement we kids would get bored and play in another part of the visitation room. As my parents would visit with my aunt, Sister Anne, the other twenty or so nuns would wander in and out to say hello. More joy and laughter, but no matter what, the greetings were limited to a hand reaching through the bars of the grille.

My sister Colleen and I would sit cross-legged, rolling a ball back and forth between us, while my brother Jimmy hovered in the corner near the grille playing with his Hot Wheels collection. When my sister and I got bored, we would wander over to the corner and begin to play with Jimmy's cars.

In the corner of the parlor was a cabinet mounted on the wall and level with a counter. My parents and all of us kids sat in the room on one side of the counter. On the other side of the grille the nuns had a counter of their own and would pull up chairs throughout the visit. Inside the cabinet was a metal cylinder that looked like a giant can of Campbell's soup. The cylinder was set up on a lazy Susan allowing it to spin around so that visitors and nuns could pass food or gifts or other items back and forth.

I don't remember what prompted my brother to do what he did that day. Jimmy was about ten then, six years older than me. I naturally looked to him for guidance and usually followed along with whatever crazy ideas he might present. So with the adults preoccupied in grown-up conversation, Jimmy lifted me up into the cabinet, set me on the lazy Susan, and closed the cabinet door. The next thing I remember was spinning around and around and around.

Immediately, I felt pulled between sheer childlike glee and unadulterated terror. Was this a game where I should be enjoying myself? Or was I too being sent behind bars for some heinous deed I didn't remember committing?

The spinning inside that cabinet seemed to last forever. Being spun around had always made me dizzy and nauseous, so I wanted Jimmy to stop me but couldn't mouth any words. Just when I hoped he had read my mind, the spinning stopped. I exhaled with a sense of relief as all three feet of me stood helpless in the dark.

Just then the doors opened. But instead of seeing Jimmy's face, Sister Anne leaned in and wrapped her arms around me. She wasn't anxious or alarmed, so neither was I.

Picture this: a group of women who will never bear their own children, who have extremely limited contact with outsiders, who have been set apart from their own relatives and siblings except for the infrequent touch of family and friends from behind the grille. Breaches in this protocol were not simply infrequent—I suspect they were unprecedented.

And by all accounts, unacceptable. After all, these nuns had taken vows to withdraw from the world. Here I was, a four-year-old kid in my devout Catholic family, and I was on the wrong side of the grille. *Behind bars with a dozen cloistered nuns.*

Even today as I recall this moment, I imagine bishops or cardinals or even the pope himself breaking into the room and catching me trespassing. In my mind their glasses are down on the tips of their noses like curmudgeonly English schoolmasters straight out of a Dickens novel.

It would take me many years to realize that my fear and anxiety about being on the wrong side and scrutinized by the religious authorities was a template for my understanding of God. If I crossed the line, God was like that displeased religious figure. If I broke the rules, God would surely break me.

But all of that fear washed away when I became aware of the joy and sense of welcome that surrounded me there. If we ambushed each other, it was an ambush of love. Sister Anne held me and ran her fingers through my hair and kissed my cheeks. This wasn't some grandmotherly cheek pinching in that patronizing kind of way. She simply took delight in who I was.

Next came Sister Jean Marie, my aunt's best friend and soulmate in the convent. Other nuns gathered around and hugged me. Sister Bernadette, born and raised in Slovakia, and who spoke with a lingering Slovakian accent, had a permanent smile on her face. Her hugs were so solid and strong, just one step short of crushing the wind out of me, but I felt so safe in her embrace, her maternal tenderness a welcome place for me to be four years old.

I don't recall which of the nuns suggested that we dance. A few small tables were pushed to the side, the nuns circled up, maybe four or five of them, and we began to sway. It started with "Ring around the Rosie" before progressing into another familiar favorite.

I still question whether we actually sang and did the hokey pokey, but the image of my preschool self dancing with a group of cloistered nuns makes me smile. Together we put our left hand in, and we put our left hand out. We put our right hand in and our right hand out. You know the rest of it: You put your whole self in, and you put your whole self out. You do the hokey pokey, and you turn yourself around.

And so, the reason my life changed that day is that from the moment of being placed into the cabinet in the container that would spin me around to the surprise of being welcomed into the arms of the nuns on the wrong side of the bars, I learned that's what it's all about.

What it's all about is an invitation to be held in loving connection. To participate in a dance where we are seen, soothed, safe, and secure. Seen as little children in our smallness and innocence.

Soothed by being held in the arms of someone stronger whose only concern is our well-being. Safe, even when we find ourselves in a container that feels disorienting and dangerous. In those moments of being seen, soothed, and safe, we also find an unexpected gift of being secure.

Looking back, I can interpret my life through that Carmel moment. That experience at the convent foreshadowed various movements of my life. The first movement, taking me into adulthood, involved that same sense of apprehension and hiding my shame. Next, I learned that life is like spinning in that cabinet, disorienting and uncertain, often confusing and unfamiliar. Finally, in recent years I have experienced the surprise of love, an awareness that when we are held and embraced securely, we somehow have everything we need no matter where we land. I realized that God delights in doing the unprecedented in order to bring us to childlike trust so that he can heal our hearts and restore our souls.

In the midst of these movements, however, I rarely saw their impact clearly.

## LOVE HAS YOU

Before I was dropped into that cabinet, I was placed into another kind of container—my family of origin. In my case this was shaped by alcoholism, emotional and sexual abuse, generations of mental illness, and shame. You see, that same year of spinning was also when my father stopped drinking for the first time. The same year my uncle began touching me inappropriately. This inauspicious legacy often limited my ability to trust and to receive love. The raw, unrelenting pain in my heart left my soul numb and kept my mind looking for answers.

You likely inherited your own generational and familial challenges. Perhaps your family maintained an image of unity and bliss to those around you but fractured into anger and abuse behind closed doors. Your parents or caregivers may have struggled with issues and addictions that hindered or incapacitated their ability to provide your basic needs, including those for attention, safety, and affirmation. You may have been forced to carry adult burdens rather than enjoy a carefree childhood.

Or perhaps your family loved and supported you well. You not only had all your basic necessities provided, but you also received emotional nourishment and parental security. And yet your story still took some turns—perhaps from choices you made or from choices others made—that now leave you confused, angry, hurt, anxious, fearful, or lonely. Regardless of your background and how you have gotten to this point, you know you want more than life has delivered so far.

So perhaps your fundamental question is similar to my own. For the last thirty years, the straightforward yet complex question shaping my life and work has remained more or less constant: How do human beings grow spiritually, emotionally, and psychologically? Basically, I want to know if people can change—if I can change—without compromising the deepest, truest part of ourselves.

Although the process is mysterious, I've concluded that, yes, we can be transformed. It's like knowing how a sailboat moves forward when wind fills the sails without knowing much about the wind. Or said another way, this transformation synchronizes with a rhythm deep within us, a rhythm I like to call God's own heartbeat.

Many people are often surprised to discover this rhythm deep within. The problem is that life itself can distract us from recognizing it. We cannot hear heaven's rhythm due to the whir of daily life. We struggle to escape from our default addictions and pain-management systems, trying to make ourselves good enough to experience God's embrace.

But what if I told you that you *could* experience that rhythm? Learn that rhythm? Live to that rhythm? And what if I told you that the rhythm is the same rhythm I discovered that day in the cabinet when I was only four years old?

That moment when the cabinet doors opened, I was brought into a welcoming circle of laughter, joy, and celebration. A circle of holiness. A circle of something wholly other, different from what I had ever known.

Love had me then, just as it has me now.

But how we get to this place is often a confusing and painful process. I recall the many clients, colleagues, friends, and acquaintances who have described their frustration, uncertainty, anger, fear, doubt, and ambivalence about spirituality, about having a personal faith.

Eileen, a campus minister at a major state university, was secretly exhausted by upholding her reputation for being "100 percent sold out for God." Beneath the surface of her public role, she was deeply disappointed with singleness. Nobody knew she took antidepressants because she was too afraid of being judged for a lack of faith. And though she never brought it up with her male superiors, Eileen felt diminished and bound by her organization's position on women in leadership.

Aaron was a Black believer who felt betrayed by the indifference his church showed in response to his experiences of racism and oppression. When he asked his pastor about starting a social justice task force to explore issues of race, Aaron was told that "a focus on social justice would minimize the proclamation of the gospel." His pastor then suggested that Aaron consider joining the choir or volunteering to work with the youth.

In seventh grade, Devin, who grew up as a missionary kid in South America, was sent off to boarding school, where he was exposed to pornography and developed a pattern of compulsive masturbation, which resulted in him becoming sexually active at a young age and at every opportunity. Growing up in a rules-based purity culture that set standards but gave little means of freedom, Devin loathed himself for his sexual sin and believed God loathed him even more.

Angelina lost her job at a prominent Christian high school in the South where she had been head of the science department. When a wealthy board member took issue with her teaching evolution, a coalition was formed to push her out for teaching "anti-biblical" views. She experienced the same kind of rejection as another client, Marco. After graduating from an evangelical seminary, he came out as gay. Suddenly he was ostracized from the faith community he had been a part of for years.

Each of these people found themselves in an unfamiliar place best described by my friend Maggie, who went through a parallel experience. "Just after graduating from a Christian college, I came to a fork in the road. I was either going to play the religious game I had known my whole life, or I was going to walk away from all that and see if my faith survived."

Maybe you have stood at a similar crossroads.

Perhaps you're there now.

Maybe you've broken the rules.

You can't play the game any longer.

You're dizzy from spinning but not sure where or if you will land.

You only know you long for a new direction.

If you have been on a similar merry-go-round of doubting, fearing, wondering, and worrying, it's time for you to discover that your faith is more than what you believe. It's meant to be a living, vibrant experience, just as real as my dance with the nuns. Come with me as we imagine together a way of being connected to ourselves—our bodies and our truest selves—as well as to God and to others. Let's explore a story that has to be imagined to be believed.

So think of this book as a compass for walking forward on your spiritual path. Together, we will explore what I've learned along the way as a licensed psychotherapist, as an ordained minister and spiritual director, and as a former professor. But mostly my guidance stems from my own struggle for a real-life relationship with God. I hope to give you a lens to see clearly, a language to engage with your own story and the stories of others, and practices for your continued passage.

There is another way of living out your faith.

There is another way of seeing the world.

There is another way that touches the deep hunger in you, honors your integrity, and ultimately gives you life from the inside out. Your heart and soul hunger for a God and a spirituality that is far better than what you've been told or experienced. And they won't let you settle for anything less.

## BLESSING

*May you open yourself to the child within.*
*May you let go of the shame that haunts you.*
*May you embrace your whole self—*
*body, mind, emotions, will, and spirit.*
*May you open your heart to the reality of being held*
*in a divine embrace.*

# 2

# DELTA

CLOSING THE GAP BETWEEN
BELIEVING AND KNOWING

*Most Christians are caught between brokenness and
ceaseless striving. Is there another way?*

DALLAS WILLARD

"I'm here to make a confession."

In my work as a psychotherapist and spiritual director, hearing someone confess is not at all unusual. For years I've boasted that I've heard it all and nothing surprises me anymore. But if this client had just confessed to leading an al-Qaeda plot to blow up the Washington Monument, I couldn't have been more surprised.

As the founding pastor of a well-known church and author of a book on church leadership, he had climbed to the top of the Christian vocational mountain, reached the peak of an exemplary ministerial career.

Impressed that he wanted to forgo preliminary chitchat and dive right in, I let him know that he had my full attention, but I wanted us to pause briefly and take three deep breaths together. We locked eyes and I waited to hear the secret burdening this man enough to visit my office.

"I believe in God . . . but I have no idea who he is."

His tone reflected the kind of guilt accompanying an admission of murder.

"Do you think this is something we can talk about?"

"Of course," I assured him. "Yes, absolutely."

Over the next several sessions I had the privilege of learning Bruce's story. He was born in the Bible Belt and from an early age was raised by his grandmother, whom he described as cold and distant, who wanted nothing more than for her grandson to be a preacher. So he did everything he thought he was supposed to do. He did everything he thought would win his grandmother's approval and affection.

"I've lived a faithful Christian life. But you know that U2 song 'I Still Haven't Found What I'm Looking For'? That's me. And you know how Jesus talked about the abundant life? I don't have a clue about that."

Bruce had baptized children and adults, preached the Bible, and led evangelistic services to share the good news of the gospel to countless people. But the good news he preached to others never landed deep in the places he needed it most—within his own heart.

"If God were to walk into the room, I don't know if I'd recognize him. I *believe* God loves me, but I've certainly never *experienced* it."

Bruce grew up in a world where conformity was valued more than relationships, where "trusting and obeying" was the currency of the faith economy defined by how God used you to bring glory to his name. He was left feeling like a successful appliance salesman. The kind that extolled the virtues of the latest and greatest appliances but whose own kitchen featured a cheap camp stove and a Styrofoam cooler from the gas station. I could relate to his struggle of not experiencing Christianity according to what I had been promised. If you're reading this book, I suspect you can relate as well.

## DELTA VARIABLE

As I sat with Bruce, I knew something of the loneliness, emptiness, and shame of his struggle. I knew how courageous it was for him to speak out loud the reality of the war within. While it has been twenty years since my double life was exposed and my world imploded, I still experience the impact of that disclosure.

Until that dismantling, my life looked together on the outside, but inside I was crippled with anxiety, depression, addiction, and doubt. I was a poster child for a successful Christian, but no one knew the real me. Nobody knew about my private addictions, the self-hatred, and my history of sexual abuse.

Looking back, I can see that the harder I tried to know God and shore up my faith by praying, serving, reading theology, and studying Scripture, the more I struggled with pornography, prostitutes, and the requisite deception to compartmentalize my transgressions. My inner turmoil and unrelenting shame remained gripped by a riptide always threatening to pull me under no matter how calmly I appeared to swim across the surface of life.

While details of our stories differed, the main themes and dynamics of my experience reflected what Bruce confided. And I know he and I are far from being the only ones. I've had the privilege of having conversations with countless souls who are struck between brokenness and ceaseless striving.

Why is there such a gap between the promises of the gospel and the reality of our lives? Why has Christianity grown so distasteful to unbelievers and irrelevant to so many believers that they are walking away from the church or from faith altogether? Why do so many believers live with a secret sense of disappointment with their experience of the Christian faith?

Regardless of the set of issues or contextual convictions in individual lives, the common denominator is a disconnect between what they believe (or once believed) and what they experience.

This gap fascinates me, and I continue to wonder if it can be closed, or at least reduced, and if so, how.

In science, the Greek letter delta is used to represent the change between a starting point and an outcome, which is why I've labeled this gap by the same name. Many of us know where we are, and we think we know what our desired outcome is. But we don't know how to get there. And we wonder if it's even possible.

My suspicion is that for a large percentage of believers who are wrestling with whether Christianity is true, the primary concern is not the veracity of their Christian belief; it's the reality of their Christian experience. The story of the gap is a source of confusion, disappointment, frustration, and pain. And far more common than we tend to realize.

The trick in life we're all trying to learn is how to live in the space between what is and what may be, what we hoped and longed for and what we've gotten, what we're meant to be and what keeps us from being all that, what we believe and what we experience. This is the gap—the delta variable.

If you are wrestling with whether Christianity is true, this book will likely leave you disappointed. I'm not writing to address the truthfulness of the Christian faith. Likewise, if you want seven easy steps to overcome the brokenness in your life, you're likely to be equally as frustrated. If you're looking for inspirational stories of triumphal faith and heroic commitment to God—well, you may want to consider a refund. But if you've already explored resources addressing these needs and found them lacking, then keep reading. You've found your tribe.

## MIND THE GAP

Bruce and the others I've described stuck in the gap seem to have three things in common. See if you can relate. First, there is *something missing* in your experience. You were promised joy, peace, freedom, purpose, and a thousand other blessings. What you experienced was shame, emptiness, weariness, pressure, and resentment.

You may often wonder how you missed what the Bible seemingly offers. Where is the abundant life to the full, the one Jesus said he came to bring? Where are the streams of living water? How can Jesus say I'll never go hungry when my heart is so ravenous? You have lost faith in a way of believing and living that seems to have overpromised but underdelivered. So you've concluded that this "too good to be true" faith is not as good as you once believed it to be.

In addition to struggling with unmet longings and expectations, those in the gap also often struggle with *something unwelcome*. You have been hurt, betrayed, abandoned, used, manipulated, diminished, and deceived. You may be struggling with relational brokenness, sexuality, pornography, mental health, and addiction. You're disenchanted with the system of faith you were taught. You're no longer willing to wear religious masks or pretend you're doing better than you actually are. Instead of helping, your experiences with Christian faith have caused harm and pain.

Consequently, like most people along the spectrum of the delta gap, you are left with *toxic or unhealthy beliefs about God*. Accepting these toxic beliefs as variables, we've then applied the laws of geometry to the ways of spirituality, and nothing could be more problematic. We want logical equations to explain, contain, and sustain our faith and our life experience.

I refer to such attempts as *dysbelief* because of this dysfunction, distinct from disbelief, which usually defines outright rejection of faith in God. These dysfunctional approaches attempt to find the key that will unlock the door into the room of abundant life. Most are flawed belief systems that pivot on causal relationships between what we do and what we should then expect to experience.

Some of the big dysbeliefs include moralism, always behaving and obeying and doing the right thing, and theologism, having the "right" theology. There's also supernaturalism, focused on preoccupation with signs, wonders, and miracles; and emotionalism, manipulating feelings to reflect what good believers should feel—namely, joy, peace, patience, and related spiritually fruity feelings. Church helpism, focused on ceaseless serving, can also fall into dysbelief.

None of these -*isms* are the problem in and of themselves. It's our human attempt to use them to force God into our geometric box. It's forcing a straight line instead of allowing for the winding road full of twists and turns and unexpected crossroads, detours, and obstacles.

It's assuming we can apply natural logic to supernatural relationship.

## HONOR WITH HONESTY

Just think about your own gap for a moment, the distance between what you think you should believe about God—how to know and relate to him—and your actual life experience. Most likely, you've had to wrestle with toxic and shame-based views of yourself. You've begun to see that the faith you once knew has required (and encouraged) you to be less human—less passionate, less honest, less curious, less engaged with reality.

You wonder if Christianity can bear the weight of your humanity and the ones you love. You're haunted by questions: Is there a place for me if I'm doubting? If I'm abused? If I'm queer? And why does it seem that in order to be more spiritual I must somehow become less than fully human? Can I ever be allowed to bring all parts of who I am?

You feel stuck in an in-between space. You can no longer accept what you inherited, but you don't have a coherent way to move forward. You're searching for an escape hatch, a treasure map, or a key to unlock the fullness of what your heart truly desires.

You need a language, a lens, some kind of new paradigm.

You're not alone. Some have already walked away from the faith and claim it's basically incompatible with who they are. Others remain in the faith but struggle to identify with the evangelical system in which they were raised. And some are in the faith but carrying brokenness that could never be addressed by their churches, pastors, and religious communities.

Increasingly, voices within the church are no longer willing to silence their own cries. They refuse to airbrush reality. They are no longer willing to pretend that their lives are better than they actually are.

They are calling BS on power-hungry leaders. They are holding church pastors accountable for emotional, spiritual, psychological, or sexual abuse. They are throwing out purity culture. They are demanding that church institutions examine how they've contributed to abuse, oppression, and racism. They are interrogating the assumptions on which their faith was founded. They are questioning the idea of Christian celebrities, whose gifting and platform overshadow their immaturity, narcissism, and emotional baggage. They are challenging traditional roles of men and women, looking at cultural and historical influences. They are questioning patriarchy and empowering women. They are insisting that the church include LGBTQ+ persons and treat them with compassion. Some are questioning the authority of Scripture.

With so much baggage, is it any wonder so few of us are deeply satisfied? So many of us are parched but still trying to slake our thirst with buying more stuff, eating more food, having more highly curated experiences, or looking at porn.

To you, and to all of us, I say: *There's another way.* There's a way of seeing the world, a way of being in the world, that touches the deep hunger in your soul and honors the grappling that life requires. That allows your soul to rest. That allows you to repair what's wrong in the world and champion justice. That allows you to bring all of your parts and pieces, no matter how broken or unwieldy. That honors faith in God with honesty about what you experience.

There is a way forward based on the best of ancient spiritual practices alongside emerging knowledge and best practices from neuroscience, psychology, attachment theory, and human development. A way forward that not only closes the gap but brings together the truth of our experience and faith.

A different kind of delta.

## RIVER TO THE SEA

*Delta* has another meaning outside of science. The delta of a river is a point where one source flows into another—a river into the sea—and the two seamlessly become one. For instance, the Mississippi River Delta is where this mighty river merges into the Gulf of Mexico.

So delta can be the gap—the distance between belief and experience. Or it can be the coming together of two separate realities, the confluence of two entities. To experience the second delta, we must name the first—a diagnosis before a treatment, if you will.

This is the journey we will explore together, from delta as distance to delta as union.

Our brokenness not as a barrier but as the bridge.

Perhaps you're skeptical or at least curious. You have questions.

You wonder, is it asking too much to experience God's loving presence in the struggles of my life? Is it unrealistic to want to be able to tell the truth about my own stories and struggles? Is it really possible to close the gap, to bridge the first delta in order to arrive at the second?

I assure you, we can close the gap and truly experience God's presence. I've walked the path myself and have witnessed the transformation in hundreds of people—friends, family, and clients. My own delta experience began when I refused to continue medicating myself with sex, alcohol, and pornography. I can also assure you that after forty years of sitting with people in the gap, you can close the delta and align the truth of your experience with what you actually believe. What seems like a contradiction is what I like to call Jesus-shaped spirituality.

You can close the delta and discover something life-giving as you cultivate Jesus-shaped spirituality deep in your body and soul. You will discover that you are already one with God, and as Martin Laird has explained, "Oneness with God is never anything we have to attain or acquire." Expounding on this idea, Laird describes how "most of us are like a person fishing for minnows while standing on the back of a whale."

You can have oneness with God in a way that honors the person you are along with your real-life struggles. You can shift from ceaseless striving and mustering faith to unforced rhythms of grace. You can bring your doubts. Your cynicism. Your questions. Your struggles. Your aversion. Your pain. Your anger. Your weariness. You are invited to bring it.

*Everything.*

## BLESSING

*May you offer yourself kindness as you attend to the gap*
*between what you believe and what you experience.*
*May you have clarity about the other way beyond ceaseless*
*striving and brokenness.*
*May you sense God's invitation to explore the*
*contradictions within.*

# 3

# ATTACHED

## BEING HELD AND BEHELD

*We all are born into the world looking for someone looking for us, and that we remain in this mode of searching for the rest of our lives.*

CURT THOMPSON

Like most new parents, I couldn't wait to hold my infant daughter.

Because my wife and I adopted her from China, because of all the hurry-up waiting we had endured, because of how quickly the tempo can change in the administrative and bureaucratic dance, my tentative anticipation only shifted to confident expectation when I landed in Beijing. Finally, all the requisite forms were completed, interviews conducted, and details concluded so I could now bring her home.

Even after I landed and began absorbing the reality that I was crossing the finish line of this patience-stretching process, I was still holding my breath, figuratively and often literally. Nothing could now overcome my determination to hold my daughter, Lily, and welcome her into our family. When that moment finally came, however, I was nonetheless unprepared for the overwhelming power of our connection.

One of our adoption counselors had emphasized the vital importance of not only holding my daughter closely and carefully, but allowing her to experience skin-on-skin contact, to hear my heart beating just as she had heard her mother's in utero. So I wanted to begin my role as a father to Lily with extra intentional care. To let go of all the challenges of the process and to embrace my baby daughter. She looked so innocent, so beautifully dependent on me and her new mom. Cradling her in my arms, gently swaying to rock her to sleep, I sensed a visceral power rising within me, a primal urge to protect her, nurture her, and defend her with my life if needed. Seeing how helpless she was, surely this was what any parent would feel.

Shortly after her arrival, however, I began to experience something completely unexpected at the opposite end of the emotional spectrum. Previously buried memories of my childhood sexual abuse surfaced and caused panic attacks as a result of post-traumatic stress disorder (PTSD). While I had already remembered more than enough of the unbearable incidents of abuse I suffered, these new memories felt exponentially worse. Memories of my uncle taking me to a smoke-filled, seedy hotel room in the city where we lived and allowing other men to use me in exchange for cash.

While the two concurrent emotional experiences—welcoming and holding our daughter as well as remembering and reacting to new horrific memories of my childhood—seemed coincidental, I eventually realized what they had in common. They both revolved around attachment.

## SEEN, SOOTHED, SAFE, SECURE

While I was aware of being abused by my uncle, I had never consciously remembered being trafficked in a rundown hotel room. Yet my body remembered even before my mind could catch up. Then as I remembered and began processing the specifics of suppressed trauma, I felt intensely vulnerable, childlike, fearful, anxious, and needy.

And what I longed for and needed as I absorbed the impact of such horrendous memories were the same four things my new baby daughter needed—to be *seen, soothed, safe,* and *secure.* My understanding of these four basic human needs has been greatly impacted by the work of Dr. Curt Thompson, a psychiatrist and author who focuses on the intersection of Christian spirituality and interpersonal neurobiology (IPNF), who credits Dan Siegel, a child psychiatrist and professor of psychiatry at the UCLA School of Medicine.

Based on their work over the past twenty-plus years, I've further developed the model of what I call the Four Ss (seen, soothed, safe, secure) as a way of understanding who we are and how we move through the world. I've found ways to describe the human needs we all experience—from cradle to grave. I'm convinced most problems disrupting our lives and impeding healthy psychological function are the direct result of how we have been seen, soothed, safe, and secure. Or, as is often the case, how those needs have gone unmet in our lives.

These four *S*-words summarize the fundamental human needs each of us experiences as newborns, as children, as adolescents, and as adults.

These needs are wired into our DNA to ensure our survival and ability to thrive in the world. We must rely on relationships with others around us in order for these needs to be met. The method and degree to which they were met when we were infants and children also determines how we learn to relate to the world around us. Or as we counselors like to say, these needs shape our ability to attach and form healthy, securely attached relationships— or not.

# THE FOUR Ss

*How being seen, soothed, safe, and secure fosters healthy attachment*

**1 SEEN**—Parent or caregiver communicates, *I get you.*
- You sensed they were engaged and attuned to you and your needs.
- You sensed you were accepted and known for who you are—and felt understood—regardless of your behavior.
- You experienced the delight of caregivers—and felt loved.
- You were given time and attention—and felt valued.
- Your thoughts, feelings, and struggles mattered—and felt welcome.

**Being *seen* lays a foundation to experience *soothing*.**

**2 SOOTHED**—Parent or caregiver communicates, *I've got you.*
- You sensed they were available and responsive.
- You experienced comfort and care when distressed, ill, or in pain.
- Your vulnerability and dependence were welcomed.
- You experienced physical and emotional affection.

**Being *soothed* promotes healthy self-soothing and experiencing *safety*.**

**3 SAFE**—Parent or caregiver communicates, *I've got this.*
- You were protected from physical and emotional danger and harm.
- You experienced repair after relational conflict or disruption.
- You had appropriate, defined boundaries (neither rigid nor unpredictable).
- You were empowered to explore, discover, and move into your world.
- You were present, connected, and confident in your body.

**Being *seen*, *soothed*, and *safe* lays a foundation for being *secure*.**

**4 SECURE**—Child experiences and internalizes, *Love has me.*
- Seen, soothed, and safe, you turned naturally toward caregivers without worry over whether you'd get what you needed.
- Your needs were met without shame.
- You could try new things and make mistakes without fear or shame.
- You knew you could relax in the strength and goodness of your caregivers.

A secure attachment is the basis for being able to trust and to have a solid sense of self, being able to experience (through your five senses) healthy intimacy whether together or apart with others in relationship. Securely attached, you practice the ability to take care of yourself as well as ask for help as needed. Curt Thompson explains, "Security is about being able, in the face of feeling seen, soothed, and safe, to move away from our relational base and step out to take the risk of new adventure, whether it's across the crib, across the room, or across the country."

The first ingredient of this secure attachment is being seen.

In its primary form, being seen is the awareness a baby has that her mother knows she is there and understands what she needs. Developmentally, a baby's eyes cannot discern depth and distance during their first few months. Initially, infants are drawn to bright colors and large shapes before recognizing the faces and expressions of the people around them. Long before babies can look into the eyes of their parent or caregiver, they know whether or not they are being seen.

Caregivers who are engaged and attuned to newborns pay attention to these tiny, dependent creatures in their care. They use soft voices, make eye contact, sing lullabies, anticipate feeding times and diaper changes. And when the child is seen, it's natural for the child to be soothed by those tending them. Soothing is about the need for comfort, for assurance, for presence, for a sense that their discomfort, pain, fear, or anxiety is recognized, acknowledged, and then remedied if possible.

So often as adults, we long to be soothed but never received healthy soothing or learned constructive ways to self-soothe as we matured. If our caregivers failed to soothe us adequately, consistently, lovingly, then by default we learned to soothe ourselves. We learned to live without soothing and to survive on our own. Our survival strategies compelled us to turn to habits, substances, and relationships to get substitutes or counterfeits for our comfort and soothing. Touching and pleasuring our own bodies, sucking our thumb or fingers, rocking ourselves, and relying on objects such as blankets or stuffed animals are some of the ways we calm and comfort ourselves when others aren't attending us, holding us, patting us, assuring us.

If we were not soothed, then our survival strategies continued through each stage of development, often predisposing us to addictions that provide quick hits of pleasure, escape from pain, and the release of endorphins and neurochemicals that calm and satiate us. Of course, there are healthy ways we can soothe ourselves—being attuned to what our body needs and providing it (nourishment? hydration? rest? exercise?), relaxing and spending time outdoors, finding physical activities we enjoy, cultivating hobbies and interests. We will explore our relationships with our bodies more in chapter five, Embodied.

Whether as infants or adults, as we draw conclusions about our needs to be seen and soothed, we begin to see how they relate to our needs for safety and security. Babies absorb the emotions of their caregivers and develop an awareness of their surroundings and any imminent dangers. Toddlers who hurt themselves because no one stopped them from touching the flame of a candle, sharp objects, or unfriendly pets form an awareness that their surroundings are harmful, painful, and dangerous. Once their autonomous nervous systems are conditioned to being tripped frequently, then their heightened nervous systems remain in fight or flight, on red alert, regardless of whether there are any actual threats.

If the need for safety goes unmet consistently, then it's likely a secure attachment will not develop. An overall sense of security remains lacking as well. If your caregivers did not see you and attune to your needs, if they failed to comfort and soothe you consistently when you experienced pain of any kind, if they could not assure your safety—or worse, harmed you themselves, directly or indirectly—then a sense of security could never develop. Security requires loving presence that is consistent and predictable.

We expect the children in our lives, such as my infant daughter, Lily, to be needy and dependent. As they mature into adulthood, however, we expect them to grow, learn, and become independent. We hold these expectations for ourselves as well. Only here's the problem: What if we have failed to grasp the extent of our secure attachment needs and the impact of how our needs were and were not met while growing up?

Please listen carefully. The way we relate to our environment, events, and other people often results more from our past conditioning than our present choosing. Our early development and family of origin profoundly affected our nervous system, which determined whether we would have a secure attachment. And that wiring is the basis for trust, including trusting in divine love.

Please pause for a moment.

If you only take away one thing from this book—and I hope you take away many more—this is the one I want you to receive. This is the source of the gap and the key to closing it. Let's unpack this idea by digging deeper into attachment styles.

### ATTACHMENT STYLES

When John Bowlby began conducting sociological research on the factors affecting mental health in the 1950s, he zeroed in on this very question: Past conditioning or present choosing? Bowlby had been trained in classic psychoanalysis as well as child and developmental psychiatry when he began working in a psychiatric hospital. Observing how children from various families and backgrounds could have such distinct and puzzling relational styles, he began to wonder more about the influence of nurture—home environment, caregiver styles, socioeconomic impact—than nature—emotional, biological, psychological variables.

Building on the studies of other doctors such as Konrad Lorenz, Bowlby narrowed his focus to separation issues between mothers and children. His studies, along with similar work by others in the field, became known as attachment theory. Today, this field continues to explore the impact our needs, and how they were met or went unmet, have on our cognitive, emotional, neurological, physical, psychological, and spiritual development. A current pioneer on this comprehensive impact is psychiatrist Curt Thompson, who explains:

> Technically, *attachment* refers to the process by which the immature infant brain accesses and utilizes the strengths of the mature adult brain in order to learn how to organize and regulate itself. Our first means of learning how to regulate our attention, memory, emotion and many other functions of the mind depends on another brain, and to some degree this continues for our entire lives. Over the course of our lives the relative health of our attachment has far-reaching implications for our flourishing, and strongly influences the eventual nature and health of the relationships we develop and maintain into adulthood.

Experts like Dr. Thompson now recognize four main styles of attachment—secure, anxious, avoidant, and ambivalent (also known as anxious-avoidant and in severe cases as disorganized). When an infant has his needs met by a mother or caregiver who is attentive, reliable, comforting, and reassuring, secure attachment develops. Healthy, secure attachment reflects all four *S*-needs being met—not perfectly but consistently and at least adequately—during one's developmental years. Securely attached adults have learned how to balance their commitment and connection to others with their individuality and autonomy.

An anxious attachment style develops when a child's needs are not met reliably enough for security and stability to develop. Those with anxious attachment may have been highly sensitive due to physiological or neurological factors, inclining them to be fussy or more difficult to soothe. Those who develop anxious attachment tend to feel insecure about their relational and emotional needs being met. They fear being rejected, abandoned, or neglected. As adults, this anxiety and insecurity can easily coalesce into people-pleasing and compromising one's wants and needs in exchange for the perceived security of their partner, spouse, family, or group.

On the other end of the spectrum, some children may have recognized their needs were going unmet and survived by meeting those needs themselves. They learned not to wait on parents or caregivers but to find ways to pacify themselves. Those with avoidant attachment styles become adults who prefer to remain independent and separate from relational attachments. This style might manifest as strength, leadership, and resilience even while keeping others at arm's length from their true emotions, needs, and desires.

The best and worst of both anxious and avoidant attachment styles converge in the ambivalent. When a child forms the belief that their needs are met sometimes but not consistently, they may respond with a push-pull style of relating. They need their Four Ss to be met reliably but don't trust they will get what they need when they need it. So they feel needy and long to be seen, soothed, safe, and secure on one hand, but on the other do not want to experience the disappointment, pain, and abandonment when their needs are ignored or neglected. Ambivalent attaching adults send mixed signals that reflect both their desire to connect and their defense against rejection or neglect.

Our attachment style (the degree to which we've been seen, soothed, safe, secure) not only shapes our human relationships; it also determines how we experience being seen, soothed, safe, and secure with God.

Please take a moment and reread that sentence.

Slowly.

What I'm saying here is that your early childhood experiences, family of origin dynamics, and the degree to which you got these foundational needs met have all shaped the gap.

If you've not been seen, soothed, safe, and secure growing up, then you will find it very difficult or it will seem impossible to know God and experience God as one who could possibly see you, soothe you, and keep you safe and secure.

## SINKING THE *TITANIC*

So the developmental attachment style you formed in your family of origin also plays out in your experience of God. After all, the Christian concept of God is inherently relational, consisting of the Trinity of three distinct persons: Father, Son, and Holy Spirit. It's not simply the struggle to view God as a lavishly doting papa when your own earthly father disappointed, abandoned, neglected, or abused you. The style of relating you developed within such familial dynamics extends to your spirituality.

In other words, no wonder you're struggling with your faith!

No wonder your beliefs and what you have been taught about God, faith, and Scripture rarely seem to align with your experience of life.

No wonder there's a gap between what you need, long for, or desire in a faith relationship with divine love and what you actually experience and receive.

No wonder rigid, harsh Christian experiences have caused such deep wounds.

Remember Bruce, the pastor? He came to see that the early loss of his parents and being raised by a cold, distant grandmother left him without the capacity and neural pathways necessary for secure attachment. His needs for the Four Ss went largely unmet. And without a reference point for a loving, nurturing parent, how could he know or experience a loving, nurturing God? He simply didn't have the neural networks in place for this kind of secure attachment to God.

Perhaps you're beginning to see the impact of your own early development.

Consider for a moment that the most shameful, regretful, horrible things you've ever done in your life are not so easily labeled "sin." What if instead of viewing yourself as fundamentally sinful, you recognized your longings and needs (those Four Ss again) as good and holy and your failures, weaknesses, mistakes, and yes, even addictions as attempts to meet those needs based on how they have gone unmet in your life? As Aquinas said, every unhealthy behavior reflects a God-given appetite—an idea which took me years to understand.

This is why attachments matter in your pursuit of a faith worth having.

Attachments are essential to what you do with your gap.

What if you could look back on your most painful, shameful moments with compassion and grace rather than self-contempt and rejection? Who would you be?

## PETER'S PEDICURE

Because being seen is so crucial to a secure attachment, this must be the starting place for closing the gap and experiencing God for who he really is. And here's the good news: Adults who find themselves with an insecure attachment can still develop a secure attachment, or what we therapists call "earned secure attachment."

We can cultivate secure attachment wherever we are today. Our neural pathways related to attachment can be rewired.

But first it's crucial to examine assumptions that may have been handed down by our family of origin and by Christian culture. Or that we perceived through survival responses and trauma. Attachments boil down to our ability to receive. An insecure attachment boils down to an inability to vulnerably receive. If our needs go unmet, we learn to limit our ability to receive throughout the rest of our lives, such as the avoidant attachment style who shuts down and withdraws from relationship, or maybe the anxious style whose survival strategy is focused on meeting the Four *S*s.

We see this resistance to receiving when Jesus washed the feet of his disciples as described in the Gospel of John. They had gathered for the Passover meal, which was their last supper together prior to Jesus' arrest and crucifixion, when Jesus humbled himself in service to make an essential point:

> Jesus knew that the Father had put all things under his power, and that he had come from God and was returning to God; so he got up from the meal, took off his outer clothing, and wrapped a towel around his waist. After that, he poured water into a basin and began to wash his disciples' feet, drying them with the towel that was wrapped around him.
>
> He came to Simon Peter, who said to him, "Lord, are you going to wash my feet?"
>
> Jesus replied, "You do not realize now what I am doing, but later you will understand."
>
> "No," said Peter, "you shall never wash my feet."
>
> Jesus answered, "Unless I wash you, you have no part with me." (John 13:3-8)

Notice that even before we're told that Jesus stood up from the table, we're reminded of the divine secure attachment Jesus had with his Father. Christ knew he had come from God and was returning to God and that the Father had put all things under his Son's power. Jesus then proceeded to serve his disciples in this deeply personal way. In a desert climate and culture where water was a precious resource, where people might go days or weeks before cleaning the dust, dirt, and grime from their bare or sandaled soles, Jesus washed the feet of each man at the table.

Only Peter wasn't having it. Allowing his Master, the Son of God, to clean his dirty feet was unthinkable—there was no way Peter would allow it. Only Jesus told Peter that if he could not receive this act of intimate kindness, then "you have no part with me." If Peter wanted to follow Christ, then he had to allow Christ to serve him in the most menial, personal way. Which was also likely soothing, comforting, relaxing.

Jesus' response was not creating conditions for their relationship. Jesus was simply describing the only way Peter could know the depths of Christ's love. Peter had to allow himself to receive in order to know the depths of love. There could be no pedigree for empowered love without Peter's pedicure.

Notice, too, in this scene that Jesus said Peter would later understand why Jesus was doing this act of love. Because within twenty-four hours, Peter would demonstrate the extremes of his relational attachment style. After expressing his willingness to follow Jesus even unto death, Peter heard Jesus foretell how Peter would deny him before morning (John 13:38). Then a few hours later in Gethsemane when the religious leaders and guards came to arrest Jesus, Peter reacted like a hothead and cut off the ear of the high priest's servant (John 18:10), which Jesus restored. And yet in only a few more hours, Peter denied even knowing let alone following Jesus (John 18:25-27).

Peter's betrayal was not the end of the story, of course. After his resurrection, Jesus appeared one morning to Peter and a half-dozen

other disciples on the beach, where he had made a fire and pre-
pared breakfast for them. Christ then reminded Peter of his loving,
secure attachment by asking Peter three times, "Do you love me?"
(John 21). Peter knew the love of Christ and could receive it, which
empowered Peter to honor Christ's request to "feed my sheep."
Peter could love others because he was securely attached to love.

## BEHOLD TO BE HELD

Sooner or later, if you're willing to be honest with yourself, you
know that your life isn't working. The life of faith you hoped to
experience seems miles away from the reality around you and
inside you. You don't deny being acquainted with Jesus, but you
don't know his love, not in the way that allows you to accept his
hands washing your feet. You wind up feeling stuck, aware of what
you long for and aware of what you can't seem to experience.

But what if through this awareness, you have the opportunity to
surrender your fears, your shame, your anxiety, your doubt, and
your despair and ask God to meet you there? Not meet you there
in a one-time, come-to-Jesus encounter that will then sustain you
for the rest of your life. In my experience, those mountaintop highs
can be magnificent, but they will not fuel your faith through all the
dark valleys still ahead.

Instead, what if you took a look at the story you've accepted as
the defining narrative of your life, the tale that gets told daily in your
thoughts, your moods, your actions, and the solace you seek for
your mishandled pain? What if you reviewed the hardest parts of
your story, the twists and turning points, and saw them more accurately, more compassionately, the way God sees you in them?

Through my own personal journey, across the lives of the hundreds of men and women I've been privileged to counsel and walk
alongside, and within the sacred history of the Christian faith, I see
the need to change how we define words like sin. Sin is basically

mishandling our pain. Defining sin through a lens of broken relationship and broken attachment leads to real healing of attachments so that we can rest and trust in a God who beholds us and loves us perfectly and unconditionally. I am convinced that the life of faith involves healing and strengthening attachments so that we can trust and rest in a God who holds and beholds us.

What if we let go of who we think we are and what we've been told we need to survive this life and instead rested in the fact that the God who looks like Jesus is actually with us in every moment of our days?

Maybe this sounds too good to be true.

If *behold* seems like an odd choice to describe how God loves you, let me explain why it's one of my favorite words in all of Scripture. In the King James Version of the Bible, *behold* appears more than a thousand times. Translated from the Greek word *eido*, *behold* literally means "be sure to see" or "take notice" or as I like to translate it, "Would you look at that!"

The God who looks like Jesus beholds us.

Holding my daughter, Lily, in my arms during her first few years of life, I loved gazing into her tiny face and radiating my biggest, goofiest smile. I loved sharing those moments of stillness when she was gazed upon and delighted in. Making those ridiculous baby-talk noises or silly sounds that emerge from adults when enraptured by the miracle of life before them. That kind of unfettered, uncomplicated joy in my child—for no reason other than my awareness of her existence in my presence—cannot begin to compare to the way our Father beholds us.

When we experience the originator of love, the essence of love, a love without strings attached, a love just because, a love existing regardless of how bad we've screwed up or fallen down in our lives, it changes everything. But again if you're reading this, you may bristle or be skeptical or ask how—how does that happen?

I respect your question and will answer it in more practical ways as we move forward. For now, though, just consider that learning to experience being held, being seen, soothed, safe, and secure in divine love is actually possible. Like learning to develop a muscle that has been atrophied, we can slowly flex and stretch. We can disconnect old default settings and grow a new capacity to receive and therefore trust love.

Years ago, there was a time when I felt numb and distant from God. In an attempt to shore up my relationship with him, I confessed in prayer that I felt like I was losing my faith. I'm sure I felt the weight of my shame and guilt because I should have been doing more to prevent my faith from slipping away. But right after telling God that I was losing my faith, I had a sense of him speaking directly to my heart: "What would be so bad about that?"

As I now understand that experience, it was my insecure attachment that prompted my fears that without my ability to muster more faith, then God was not only disappointed with me but wanted nothing to do with me. Only, that experience was not about the strength of my faith. It was about the insecurity of my attachment to God. My body and my nervous system had not learned to trust love based on the way my needs went mostly unmet during my childhood.

Just as Peter was initially unable to imagine receiving the gift of Jesus' love by allowing his Master to wash his feet, I couldn't imagine that losing faith as I knew it might be a good thing. But what I was losing had nothing to do with my beliefs, my passion, and my desire to know God. It had to do with my efforts, my ceaseless striving, my exhaustion and weariness. Sometimes we must lose what we have been clinging to and calling our faith in order to receive God's love, in order to allow him to wash our feet, to experience divine secure attachment.

This is a lot to consider. You may have been longing for a more authentic faith for a long time but have nonetheless held on to the familiar habits of your own efforts. It's what comes natural based on the unmet needs you're carrying. It's what you've learned from the Christian culture and your faith experiences. But if you want to close the gap and experience a faith worth living, then it may be time to try something new.

**BLESSING**

*May you recognize how your need to be seen, soothed,*
*safe, and secure has shaped your life.*
*May you connect the dots between your unmet needs*
*and how you have tried to meet them.*
*May you embrace these needs as God-given and their*
*fulfillment as essential to closing the gap.*
*May you open your heart to receive divine love*
*that meets these basic needs.*

4

# EVIL

REJECTING THE LIES ABOUT GOD
AND ABOUT OURSELVES

*Evil is live spelled backwards.*

M. SCOTT PECK

Most of us experience evil before we know how to name it.

When I was about four, I encountered evil in the basement of a bar in the neighborhood where we lived. By some miracle, I have never remembered specific images. But for nearly three years, I experienced what are known as body memories. When my body reacted as if the trauma was happening again and manifested the physical symptoms. If this is something you've experienced, then please be cautious as you read the following paragraphs as well as this chapter. You may need to stop and take a break or skip ahead.

Those somatic memories can still haunt me. A bare lightbulb glowed above me, dangling from the rafters. The damp room smelled of stale beer from the cases of empty amber bottles and drained kegs lining the walls, along with a whiff of mold and mildew. I could hear muffled voices and the hum of a jukebox from the floor above us.

And despite not knowing exactly what was taking place, I somehow felt complicit.

If this scene makes you uncomfortable, please understand that I have spared the graphic details, the ones burned into my mind and body and still smoldering more than fifty years later. I understand that while virtually everyone condemns the abuse I experienced in that basement, few want to know specifics and look into the face of evil. And I suspect you have your own encounters with evil from which to define and describe the sheer absence of goodness. While yours may not be as direct or shocking as mine, they might also be much worse.

The thing about evil, though, is that a little goes a long way.

Cancer, poison, venom—choose the metaphor that helps you understand that evil cannot be quantified. That it relies instead on quality, intensity, consistency, and density. Like a microscopic particle undetectable to the naked eye, evil travels in search of chain reactions to ignite so that it can multiply. And leave destruction in its wake.

## TEMPTED IN THE DESERT

Evil is one of those concepts that we inevitably identify from a distance—torture, abuse, suffering, genocide, mass murder, terrorist attacks, war crimes—but struggle to see how it plays out in our own lives. As an abstraction, evil often seems to exist removed from the direct personal impact it has in our lives. It's out there somewhere, often embedded in the vices of others such as greed or lust or gluttony. As an entity, evil resides in the supernatural, a malevolent force intent on harm, destruction, chaos, confusion. As a moral category, evil usually reflects the lack of value placed on human life, on justice, on cooperation, compassion, and kindness.

Evil is also often used synonymously with *wicked*, but the two are actually distinct. When used as nouns, evil means moral depravity or immorality, whereas wicked means people who are depraved or immoral. When used as adjectives, evil means intending to harm or destroy with or without rationale, whereas wicked means harmful, from mischievous to murderous, by nature.

The crucial difference between the two, for me at least, is the goal. Evil always seeks to destroy beauty and goodness with two lies—by deceiving us about who God is and who we are. Wickedness yields to temptation in order to experience what it lacks—assuming God can't or won't provide what feels necessary to live.

One of the best pictures God gives us of evil emerges in the temptations Jesus faced from the devil. Wanting to fast and pray, Jesus goes to the desert alone and does not eat for forty days. At the end of this time, the devil tries to exploit Christ's weakened physical condition.

But there's another important aspect of their encounter. Prior to fasting and praying in the desert for forty days, Jesus had been baptized by John. As he came up from the water, "heaven was opened, and he saw the Spirit of God descending like a dove and alighting on him." And then God's voice blessed Jesus: "This is my Son, whom I love; with him I am well pleased" (Matthew 3:16-17).

Knowing what Jesus would face in the desert, his Father made sure that his Son knew he was seen, soothed, safe, and secure.

And Jesus would need to remain securely attached to his Father in order to resist the devil's temptations. First, the enemy seems to appeal to the hunger of someone who has fasted for forty days: "If you are the Son of God, tell these stones to become bread" (Matthew 4:3). Basically, the devil offers Jesus a way to be soothed. Knowing Christ is famished from his fast, the tempter tries to bait Jesus into using his power in a way that meets his own needs rather than relying on the love of his Father. It's the same temptation we face between our own unhealthy self-soothing and being known and loved by God and others.

But there's another, covert temptation embedded in the devil's suggestion, which attempts to undermine who Jesus is, his very identity as the beloved Son of God, by casting doubt with one little word: "*If* you are the Son of God . . ." On one hand this is ludicrous, but when we're suffering, we often remain unseen. The same way I was not seen in my abuse, or my clients were not seen when suffering the various traumas they've endured. Then we don't want to be seen in our pain and vulnerability, so we create masks to hide behind.

But Jesus knew who he was and replied, "It is written: 'Man shall not live on bread alone, but on every word that comes from the mouth of God'" (Matthew 4:4). So the devil moves on from soothing to safety:

> Then the devil took him to the holy city and had him stand on the highest point of the temple. "If you are the Son of God," he said, "throw yourself down. For it is written: 'He will command his angels concerning you, and they will lift you up in their hands, so that you will not strike your foot against a stone.'" (Matthew 4:5-6)

Once again, it sounds like a demonstration of God's divine protection and provision, and the devil cloaks this in religious language. Evil likes to sound as close to the truth as possible. Evil will always present alternatives to meeting our deep needs and take us away from the vulnerability of love.

Jesus handles it once again by quoting from the Scriptures: "It is also written: 'Do not put the Lord your God to the test'" (Matthew 4:7). Rather than trusting God with our safety and security, we may unintentionally test him by claiming biblical verses or passages as promises for our present circumstances. Instead of finding that God meets us where we are—in the midst of our pain, shame, and discomfort—we may feel spiritually entitled to a smoother journey.

Finally, there's the temptation to experience ultimate security. Having failed with these previous two attempts, the devil goes all in. Looking down from a high mountaintop offering panoramic views of manmade kingdoms, the devil declares, "All this I will give you . . . if you will bow down and worship me" (Matthew 4:9). Basically, it's an offer to shift allegiance—renouncing God and worshiping Satan—in exchange for worldly power, riches, authority, celebrity, and luxury. Rather than face suffering, torture, and death, Jesus could rest easy with the world at his feet, literally.

We face this temptation in our attempts to define and empower ourselves through what we worship. I've heard it said that worship is what we give our hearts to in exchange for life. I would add that worship is what we give our hearts to in exchange for security, in exchange for being seen and soothed and safe. We can worship what we do, how much we earn and acquire, and who we know, all in attempting to meet our own four S-needs, which is the essence of idolatry.

Jesus does not yield to the devil's temptations, but rather than engage in a power struggle, God's beloved Son uses the power of truth: "Away from me, Satan! For it is written: 'Worship the Lord your God, and serve him only'" (Matthew 4:10). As the Word made flesh referenced in John 1, Jesus embodies the truth of the Scriptures he quotes. Living in the power of truth sets us free from the lies and deceptions of the enemy.

Truth is not a proposition. It's all of reality aligned with who God is. When a wheel's spokes are out of alignment, they are said to be "out of true." Until we know and experience the holiness of God, we remain out of true, off-kilter, and out of balance. We cannot be fully whole until we realize we are fully holy.

The truth of our own story within the truth of God's story draws us back to love.

Truth is our weapon over evil.

Truth illuminates the enemy's lies and deception.

Truth sets us free.

## ONE-SIDED RELATIONSHIPS

For several years I was a professor at a local seminary, and among the courses I taught was a graduate level class to train students, mostly pastors and counselors, in treating addictions. Every semester I began the class the same way: "What is an addiction? What's the difference between an addiction and a compulsion? What's simply a bad habit that we need to change versus an uncontrollable behavior causing destruction?"

After much lively discussion, several definitions of addiction emerged. Several students provided clinical descriptions drawn from the latest edition of the *Diagnostic and Statistical Manual of Mental Disorders*, the professional bible of mental health treatment. Other definitions arose from a biblically based understanding of addictions, usually based on their understanding of sin and not particularly helpful. Near the end of that first class, I would present two definitions in the mix that, together with the ones students offered, would guide the remainder of the semester.

Like two separate lenses in a pair of glasses, these definitions of addiction invited students to see the soul of a person. The first one is my paraphrase of John Bradshaw's description of addiction as an unhealthy mood-altering relationship with a person, substance, or behavior. This definition is my favorite because it emphasizes one's relationship with addictions and compulsions. We don't typically think about them this way, but it reveals the problem. If someone asks whether you're currently in a relationship, you probably wouldn't say, "Why, yes, I am. I'm currently committed to ice cream and gelato," or, "Yes, I'm in a long-term relationship with a wonderful man named Jack. Perhaps you know him—Jack Daniel's?"

The point here is that a healthy relationship is inherently reciprocal and mutually beneficial. With our addictions, however, the person, substance, or behavior—which promises to give us so much at first—eventually starts to take from us. Until it takes everything.

The second definition is much simpler and more concise: addiction is spinning in place. This definition is clearly more ambiguous and encompassing, and perhaps that's why I like it. Because each of us will go through periods of spinning in our lives. We will be going about whatever we're doing each day when life no longer seems to work. It may be sudden and abrupt due to illness, injury, betrayal, or loss. Or it may be gradual and cumulative, a slow tide eroding our thoughts and emotions.

So we begin spinning, grasping at something to provide comfort, distraction, pleasure, and relief. In his book *Spirituality of the Psalms*, theologian Walter Brueggemann wrote about life's rhythm being oriented, disoriented, and reoriented. Richard Rohr's book *The Wisdom Pattern* described the cycle in terms of order, disorder, and reorder. My former pastor spoke of it in terms of thrive, dive, and revive. Regardless of how we name it, the spinning is the same. It boils down to coming up against an experience that stops us, shakes us, hurts us, humiliates us, redefines us.

It may be a cancer diagnosis or the loss of a spouse. It may be losing your job during a pandemic or losing your apartment to eviction. It may be that you had an affair and derailed your marriage. Whatever it is, you're left spinning, orbiting around whatever has enough gravity to pull you away from the terrible pain.

During the darkest and lowest days of my addictions, just one or two choices could have set me on a course of evil from which I likely would not have turned back.

I remember a number of dark moments during the lowest days of my addiction when I was given opportunity to cross lines that I now find unthinkable. Looking back, I'm forever grateful that despite the extent of my struggles, there were still lines that I didn't cross.

## TWO CORE LIES

Evil is sustained by two essential lies. One is about God: you can't trust God to meet your needs. And the other lie is about who you are: it's up to you to meet your own needs so you must find a way. Or said another way:

1. You can't trust God.

2. It's up to you because God won't come through.

Every sin I've committed or someone has committed against me has been fueled by these two lies. Every world problem . . . these two lies have made the world go around for all of time.

The name I've given to this path and process is the rhythm of the kingdom. When our eyes are open—which usually happens only when we're spinning and disoriented—we begin to see the rhythm of the kingdom on every page in Scripture. All the way back in the beginning it was God's way. Adam and Eve were experiencing life going well. They got everything they needed. They had each other so they were not alone, and they went for walks with God every day.

They're unaware of how perfectly their needs are met—the knowledge that love has them—because all they know is the security of being in paradise while in relationship to each other and to God. They're given free rein to create meaning in beauty and enjoyment, in naming and exercising their dominion, in discovery of the pleasures of their senses. They are oriented and securely attached—they fully have their bearings. They know who they are, where they are, and whose they are. But then they started to spin.

Adam and Eve were already aware of the only prohibition God had given them: not eating the fruit from a certain tree among the countless branches weighted with delicious bounty. Then they hear a whisper that perhaps this limitation means their needs are not being fully met after all. Seeds of doubt watered by the enemy's lies take root. Lies that questioned whether they were really seen, soothed, safe, and secure.

As doubt blossoms into disbelief of the truth, they lose their bearings. They reach out and grasp life on their own terms. Their eyes are opened to a new and different reality; they now know evil.

But in their spinning and disorientation, God came looking for them.

Significantly, the first words out of God's mouth are not words of criticism, chastisement, or condemnation. They are words of reorientation: "Where are you?" (Genesis 3:9). In the words of Bob Dylan, Adam had "no direction home"—he and Eve were, in fact, hiding. How God responded to his human creations reminds me of my response to my son shortly after he had just gotten his driver's license. In his maiden voyage on the interstate, his trusty Subaru died. Going almost seventy miles per hour, the engine just stopped, so he coasted to the left shoulder with vehicles speeding by only inches away. When he called and explained, my first response was "Where are you?" As a dad I needed to know he was safe.

Adam and Eve similarly coasted into new territory after allowing evil to poison their innocence. They no longer recognized who they were and where they were. So God began by reorienting them.

One of the effects of spinning is that we lose our sense of where we belong, where home is for our soul. We're disconnected from an inner sense of safety and security. We feel alone. Our distress is palpable. For many of us, our childhood home was a place of pain and loss and even trauma and unpredictability. A place you wanted to leave and never return. A place from which to escape.

As a result, we separate from the deep longing for a good home, a safe shelter for our souls, a place of warmth, acceptance, and comfort. Consequently, we avoid dependency in connection. We cut off the need for others. Oh, we may be extroverted, or be in a committed relationship. But deep within we avoid what we want the most. Others may experience a Do Not Disturb sign as they try to enter into relationship with you. If they manage to walk through the door, you run and hide or push them out again.

Or perhaps your response to the pain or absence of home has been an attempt to recreate home within. When we attempt to re-create home, we're looking for that sense of satisfaction that's temporarily provided by our addiction or compulsion. Geneen Roth confirms, "Compulsion is about the sense that no one is home." Basically, we vacate ourselves because it's too painful to remain present and face the loss, the grief, the woundedness. So whether it's food or sex or drink or shopping or people-pleasing, we obsessively pursue a substance or person, behavior or object that will allow us to feel a sense of relief and belonging, a moment of home.

The problem is that as the cycle of compulsion gets sparked, the proverbial porch light comes on. Compulsion, and its cousin addiction, always leave the light on for us. It beckons and draws us, invites us—welcome, here's a safe place we can go. We can enter into a place where all the pain fades away . . . at least for a little while. As singer-songwriter David Wilcox attests in his song "Eye of the Hurricane," "When you lay your dream to rest, you can get what's second-best. But it's hard to get enough."

Time after time, we drive to the curb and the light is still on. We open the car door and walk up the front steps. We open the door, and all at once see candles flickering in the warm glow. Scented with our favorite fragrance. Fresh bread is baking in the oven. We may even hear the voices of loved ones calling: Come on in. Bring your heart. Bring your fear. Bring your hunger and emptiness. Your heart quickens. And then, and then . . .

Every single compulsion and addictive act ends with these words: and then . . .

And then take a drink. And another one. And then just one more. Look at these bodies and those. And then you can join them.

Hit Return and complete the purchase. And then . . .

Visit the ATM and overdraw another account. And then you'll win it all back.

Evil thrives on the mantra "and then . . ."

Evil fills the gap between our woundedness—all that has hurt us, disappointed us, been lost to us, injured us, abandoned us—and our wandering (sometimes referred to as sin), that longing to settle for fantasy rather than suffer for reality.

## CLOSING THE GAP

The work of closing that gap takes place at the intersection of our woundedness, weakness, and warfare, which we'll discuss more in chapter six. For now, consider—Will we allow doubts and distrust to take root and flourish? Or will we move into greater wholeness by learning to trust, by inviting God and other people into the wilderness where we find ourselves far from home?

Our wounds and vulnerabilities create a landing pad for evil that can become a launching pad for our unhealthy, counterproductive behaviors (what we commonly call sin) in our lives. When we accept the bondage of addiction and idolatry, we blind ourselves to the way evil feeds off all the pain we feel. It's much easier to cultivate anger and justification than grief and lament. If we're willing to seek healing for our wounds rather than resigning ourselves to them, and if we're willing to steward our vulnerabilities into connection with others instead of self-sufficiency, we will be on our way to experiencing wholeness.

Simply put, our vulnerabilities, hurts, and wickedness can propel us toward God or away from him toward the allure of evil. And evil is alluring. The enemy of our souls knows what appeals to us and why those places within us are tender and vulnerable. The evil one knows we long to be known and loved and accepted, to belong and feel at home, to have a purpose that matters more than our own comfort and convenience.

But the enemy's power is limited.

While God's power is unlimited. And fortunately that power is displayed most regularly in weakness and woundedness, not by divine flexing.

God's superpower is his never-ending kindness.

And whether you believe the Bible or not, or consider the devil the spiritual source of evil, it's hard to deny that painful obstacles always seem to pop up. Regardless, the Bible warns us to take the enemy seriously: "Be alert and of sober mind. Your enemy the devil prowls around like a roaring lion looking for someone to devour" (1 Peter 5:8).

Countering the presence of evil in our lives is often called spiritual warfare, which may sound silly or overly militaristic or hyperbolic. But if you have faced your struggles, addictions, trauma, adversity in your family of origin, then you know that warfare is not an overstatement. "For our struggle is not against flesh and blood, but against the rulers, against the authorities, against the powers of this dark world and against the spiritual forces of evil in the heavenly realms" (Ephesians 6:12).

Evil seeks to pinpoint your pain and force you to experience it just enough to want relief, comfort, escape, or others to blame, hate, or take vengeance on. If evil can convince you that you're a victim, basically powerless against what it can provide, then you lose sight of who you are and who God is. Which is why the evil one confuses and destroys. His methods rely on lies, doubts, omissions, and exaggerations, the same bag of deadly tricks he's always used, whether tempting Eve and Adam in the garden or Jesus in the desert.

To overcome evil, you must identify the lies that create the big lie—that love does not have you. You must see these lies and replace them with what is true and reflects the reality you know is there but cannot always be seen.

Knowing the truth sets you free (John 8:32). The truth filters out the lies, assumptions, false narratives, and exaggerated emotions that keep us stuck in our brokenness.

The only power evil has is in relationship to our choices. Consider how a spark ignites oxygen to produce a flame. In and of itself, the spark does not have the power to enflame, but if oxygen is close enough, the spark ignites it into a blaze. Similarly, our passion and desire get sparked and ignited in our brokenness.

Sin is the result of turning from divine love. Repentance is turning toward that same love, then realizing that love has been holding us all along. Overcoming evil means closing the gap and realizing nothing can pull you away from the love that has you. "Who shall separate us from the love of Christ? Shall trouble or hardship or persecution or famine or nakedness or danger or sword? . . . No, in all these things we are more than conquerors through him who loved us" (Romans 8:35-37).

Evil wants you to believe the lie that love does not have you.

But the truth is that love will always have you.

## BLESSING

*May you recognize and refute the lies, deception,*
*and accusations of evil in your life.*
*May you know the truth that sets you free*
*and opens the eyes of your heart.*
*May you see what is real—about who you are*
*and about who God is.*

*5*

# EMBODIED

## CONNECTING TO OUR BODIES
## AND CONNECTING TO GOD

*The first inner territory of the spiritual journey is the body.*

JACK SHEA

Exactly one day after graduating seminary, Geoffrey became an atheist.

A man in his midthirties, he revealed this decision while sitting across from me in my counseling office. After some initial pleasantries to break the ice, I had asked how I could be of help, and his delivery rivaled the nuanced emotions of an Academy Award–winning actor—a blend of resigned sadness, simmering rage, numbed desperation, and courageous pride.

"Wow," I said, pausing to acknowledge the dissonance and loss conveyed by his statement. "I'm guessing you didn't become an atheist overnight, though. How would you describe your relationship with God when you entered seminary?"

Our conversation unfolded from there, as Geoffrey described how he had grown up in a fundamentalist Christian environment, earned a bachelor's degree at a well-known Christian university, and then joined the military. Serving as an intelligence specialist in Afghanistan, he often sat outside his unit's bunker and watched the war on terror play out only feet away. Although he incurred no physical injuries, the impact on his emotions and internal world shattered the veneer of the comfortable faith he had inherited growing up. So when he returned and was honorably discharged, Geoffrey enrolled in seminary to shore up his fragile faith. Geoffrey experienced what the military as well as clinicians call "moral injury."

"I needed something to anchor me, and that's when I defaulted back to God—at least, I thought that's what it was. I was just so desperate for my life to have meaning, you know? Faith provided that for a while . . . and I thought going to seminary would solidify what I believed. Learning more about theology, the Scriptures, and the history of the Christian church should have given me more confidence . . . but instead my doubts started multiplying."

"Did you discuss your doubts with anyone—other seminarians, your professors, your family or friends?"

Geoffrey suppressed a laugh and cut his glance away from me, shaking his head. "Yeah, I tried . . . but no one wanted to hear about doubting God. What if it was contagious? So I didn't really bring it up anymore. I kept thinking that one day everything would fall into place. I studied harder than anyone. I prayed. Devoted myself to the Scriptures. I actually won the preaching award given by faculty; can you believe that?"

"How did that feel to be recognized for your preaching?"

"Like playing the performance of a lifetime. That's why I had to stop pretending, quit performing . . ."

And that's why he stopped believing in God.

"The more I tried to suppress or compartmentalize my doubts and uncertainties, the more stressed I became. I started experiencing health problems—migraines, digestive problems, muscle spasms, insomnia. So I told myself that I would finish my seminary degree and then make a decision about what to do. The day after graduation, I woke up from sleeping through the night for the first time in months and I immediately knew what was true. My body had been trying to tell me for a long time. I admitted what had once been my greatest fear: that I don't believe in God. The more I tried to find him, the further I got from experiencing a sense of his presence . . . until there was nothing left."

"So why did you come to see me today, Geoffrey? It sounds like you finally have the resolution you've been wanting."

He stared into the dappled green, shadowed treetops beyond my third-story windows.

"I . . . I'm not sure. I just feel . . . lost . . . hollow inside . . ." Deep sigh.

"Where do you experience this lost, hollow feeling in your body? Where does it reside physically?"

He returned his gaze to me and leaned forward like a curious child. "My chest, maybe. The tightness I felt all during seminary is looser. Sometimes now I feel a little dizzy . . . almost hungover." Geoffrey shrugged. "Maybe I'm grieving what I used to believe, what I hoped to find in seminary."

"What if that's okay? What if that's necessary to discover what's next?"

His head tilted as if bearing the weight of my questions.

"What if you simply need to be an atheist right now in order to find God?"

## MICROSCOPE OR TELESCOPE

On one level Geoffrey's crisis sounds like the result of numerous variables, including complex PTSD, which of course it is. Considered from a simpler perspective, however, his dis-ease is basically the same one experienced by almost every client who walks into my counseling office. The symptoms manifest differently, but the same cause is at the root.

Whether a crisis of faith, a battle with addiction, sexual brokenness, or depression and anxiety, for hundreds of years, the tendency among Christians has been to view such problems as the result of our sinful nature, a spiritual battle with the enemy, a power struggle between individual will and divine surrender. Regardless of symptoms—painful emotions, intrusive thoughts, physical distress—the remedy prescribed a singularly spiritual treatment, primarily some variation of Bible study and prayer.

The problem with this paradigm is that it doesn't work.

If it did, then people wouldn't continue to struggle with overcoming addictions, repeating harmful patterns of behavior, and wounding themselves and others relationally. If we only needed to know more about the meaning of the Bible in order to understand and apply it, then I wouldn't be writing this book and you wouldn't have wanted to read it. You wouldn't need to. You could spend your time instead reading devotionals, prayer guides, and inspirational exposition of Scripture. You could attend seminary or explore religious studies at the nearest university.

Please understand I'm not discounting the value and impact of those means, messages, and methods. But the fact remains that no matter how much we long to obey God's commandments and guidelines, no matter how often we try to resist temptation, no matter how much we learn or study or pray, it's not enough. At certain intervals we hit a wall and suddenly realize we're only spinning our wheels. Life on a treadmill, one that seems rigged against our ability to step off and walk in a new, distance-spanning, gap-closing direction.

The problem with a paradigm of striving and trying harder, of performing and attempting to please God, is that it doesn't touch where we live. It's not compelling in moments of pain, in dark nights of fear and anxiety, in instances of intense craving, in caverns of loneliness.

Instead of viewing our sinful behaviors under a microscope, we need to study the expansiveness of how God made us through a celestial telescope. This is not merely my opinion. We see this revealed in the sprawling story of God.

You may be wondering where this macro-focus emerges in the Bible. Where in the Bible do we find this more comprehensive, cohesive focus on how we're made? Simply put, it's contained in the biblical idea of soul.

While the word *soul* is often overused, it is important that we clarify and grasp its impact. Many beliefs and assumptions about the human soul result from references in the New Testament, which reflects the Greek understanding of soul as one's mind, emotions, and will. This emphasis is what we've been left with in Christianity as we know it.

But the Hebrew concept of the soul found in the Old Testament is more comprehensive and encompasses the mind, emotions, will—and body.

In order to connect with God and experience what it means to be seen, soothed, safe, and secure with him, we must come back to this ancient idea of the soul, with its emphasis on our embodied self. The soul is designed to experience shalom, not simply peace but wholeness, integration of the body, mind, emotions, and will. All of you.

Digging deeper in the Old Testament, we find the Hebrew word *nephesh* conveys the holistic connection and containment of the mind, body, and heart. Appearing just shy of seven hundred times, *nephesh* tends to be translated with more variety than most other ancient words because the concept encompasses so many facets of our humanity. We often find it rendered as soul, the essence of oneself and personhood:

> Let my soul live and praise you,
> and let your rules help me. (Psalm 119:175 ESV)

My soul thirsts for God,
for the living God. (Psalm 42:2 ESV)

Other English translations for *nephesh* include heart, life, living
being, desire, emotion, and will. Sometimes it emerges in the
choice of personal pronoun, such as *I* and *myself*. While most trans-
lators rely on the context to guide their selection, it's clear that the
entirety of who we are as human beings created in the image of God,
*imago Dei*, emerges.

In New Testament Scriptures, the Greek word *psychē* closely
parallels the meaning of *nephesh*, describing distinct yet connected
internal personal parts responsible for feeling, thinking, choosing,
and acting. It's the sense of wholeness expressed by Jesus in stating,
"You shall love the Lord your God with *all your heart* and with *all
your soul* and with *all your mind*. This is the great and first com-
mandment" (Matthew 22:37-38 ESV, my emphasis).

You may be thinking, "That's great, but doesn't this just reinforce
that our struggles in life are always fundamentally a spiritual problem?'"

Yes, it does—but not *just* a spiritual problem.

Our struggles also reflect a physical problem.

An emotional problem.

A cognitive problem.

A neurological problem.

When soul is considered through this Hebrew lens, we discover
that all of these are spiritual. The body is the context in which the
spirit operates. We cannot separate the spiritual and the emotional.
God is certainly both. Created in his image, our spirit operates
within our human body. With the incarnation of Jesus, God fully
experienced living in the form of his human creation.

The solution for our spiritual struggles then emerges where they
all intersect.

This point of intersection? *Embodiment.*

## GOOD IS BETTER THAN PERFECT

The shift from the Hebrew understanding of soul to the more limiting Greek idea has resulted in a kind of dualism, an either-or assumption about who we are in relation to who God is. This dualism tells us that we are flawed and broken while God is holy and perfect. Therefore, we're separated from him by our vast imperfections.

But that's the problem then: We can never achieve perfect . . . can we?

This dilemma with perfection lingers for us still. On any given day we're well aware of how far from perfection we remain . . . to the point that attempting perfection seems impossibly futile. When we're in touch with our brokenness, perfection taunts us with its pristine holiness, which in turn usually trips shame for all the ongoing imperfections in our lives. We will never achieve anything close to the perfection of God's holiness—more about this in the next two chapters—so why try harder?

But what if we've been viewing perfection all wrong—in large part thanks to false assumptions and misunderstanding the truth about perfection? What if perfection is not about some flawless, sinless, static state to be attained but an integrated sense of wholeness that's continually growing, changing, maturing?

Throughout the Bible, God is not known by his perfection but by his goodness. Going back to creation in Genesis, after each new form came into being, God pronounced that it was good—not perfect. And this was *prior* to Adam and Eve disobeying God and activating the sinful consequences of being able to choose how we live. Clearly, goodness and perfection are not the same.

Brian McLaren summarizes this key difference by concluding, "Hebrew good is better than Greek perfect. In other words, Greek *perfect* is static, but Hebrew *good* is dynamic. Greek *perfect* is sterile and changeless, but Hebrew *good* is fertile and fruitful."

Considering Jesus' command to "be perfect" (Matthew 5:48), we see how this echoes his description of our relationship with him and with the Father: "I am the vine; you are the branches. If you remain in me and I in you, you will bear much fruit; apart from me you can do nothing" (John 15:5). It's no coincidence that Christ chose an organic metaphor, one that's not only familiar to his agrarian original audience but that aptly expresses the dynamic nature of becoming transformed by the power of his Spirit within us—within our *bodies*.

## SCORE KEEPING

Putting these pieces together, we gain an understanding of the vital importance of embodiment. In his groundbreaking book, *The Body Keeps the Score*, Bessel van der Kolk explores the ways trauma manifests physically, emotionally, biologically, and neurologically. He concludes what the Bible has been telling us all along: we cannot separate, segregate, fragment, or compartmentalize one major aspect of ourselves from all the rest. At least, not indefinitely.

Van der Kolk describes how the majority of individuals diagnosed with PTSD have temporarily stored the impact of their life's traumatic experiences in their body. And as his title emphasizes, the body not only does not forget but keeps score, registering and often repeating our responses to trauma until we consciously integrate and process the traumatic experiences. He explains:

> We have learned that trauma is not just an event that took place sometime in the past; it is also the imprint left by that experience on mind, brain, and body. This imprint has ongoing consequences for how the human organism manages to survive in the present. Trauma results in a fundamental reorganization of the way mind and brain manage perceptions. It changes not only how we think and what we think about, but also our very capacity to think.

Thanks to the work of Van der Kolk and other leading researchers, our understanding and definition of trauma has also changed. Initially, trauma described the combat experiences of military veterans, the life-threatening danger faced by law enforcement, the injuries of crime victims, and the shock of survivors in natural disasters and major crises. Neurologists studying the brain's response to various catalysts, however, learned that the trauma impact is often the same regardless of the severity or actuality of danger.

In the embodied moment the body keeps the score.

When we expand our understanding of the soul to include the body, the expansion becomes a window.

So our understanding of soul must include the body.

When we hold the physical and spiritual together, we realize that there is no score keeping. This is a good thing because where there is score keeping, there is a winner and a loser, a good guy and a bad guy—hearkening back to Gnostic dualism. Embodiment holds all aspects, even the contradictory and problematic ones, within the tension of both-and rather than the fragmentation of either-or. There is a belief originating in the early church that the body is bad and the spirit is good, separating and value labeling body and spirit.

When we ignore bodies and physical sensations, including our desires and appetites that we're often quick to label sinful and attempt to distance ourselves from feeling, then we compound our struggle. When we experience traumatic situations, our bodies go into survival mode, the fight, flight, freeze, or faint responses. What often happens, however, is that our responses get lodged and suspended, compartmentalized and pushed aside.

We push through the trauma because of our innate survival response, but that survival response leaves something unprocessed. Something happens to you that gets stuck and separated from the way you normally move through and integrate memories, feelings, and thoughts.

We do what we have to do in order to survive the danger, the abuse, the combat, the injury, the betrayal, the loss, the trauma. Rather than receiving the messages being conveyed by our body and its physical, biological, and neurological signals, we are hard-wired to temporarily separate them—and eventually suffer their segmentation. The brain reacts to the perceived threat and experienced trauma with compartmentalization.

This is why my client Geoffrey experienced so many physical ailments that escalated as he continued in seminary. It wasn't simply that his body was trying to tell him that he didn't really believe in God. His body was trying to highlight the dissonance between what he actually believed compared to his everyday experiences, including his two years of life-threatening everyday experiences while serving in Afghanistan.

His somatic symptoms reflected a comprehensive, holistic problem that affected all parts of his being, including his spirit.

Geoffrey's body kept the score, dominating his mind and emotions, and particularly limiting his willpower.

## CRUCIAL COMPANION

So what was actually going on with Geoffrey? Not only did he suffer a kind of moral injury or faith crisis—he was suffering PTSD, which continued to manifest in his body.

His trauma communicated that a major disconnect had occurred within his various internal systems. His brain recorded data but struggled to process experiences at odds with his beliefs. Something had to give in order to make sense of the trauma, which led Geoffrey to let go of his long-held faith beliefs. And yet his body continued to express physical symptoms of the still-unprocessed trauma.

While our brains serve as a supervisory analyst and regulatory governor of our bodily experiences and sensory data, the brain is still *part of our body*, an organ connected to all other bodily systems and functions. Our brains fundamentally operate in a bicameral system with two hemispheres, left and right, working together to cover all bases within how we live, feel, think, decide, act, remember, respond, and react. Generally speaking, the left brain houses neurological systems focused on data, information, patterns, repetition, logic, and certainty. The right contains areas tasked with possibility, receptivity, creativity, and attachment.

Geoffrey's problem reflects the same disembodiment we often experience with regard to our faith. He wanted something solid, substantial, reliable, unchangeable, true. Consequently, he rediscovered his Christian faith and systematically pursued it with a scholar's passion.

His body, though, was keeping the score.

The problems he began to notice resulted from his trauma and resulting numbness. Because his body was keeping the score, he was unable to doubt, to feel, to explore, to be curious and open. His body needed certainty rather than vulnerability.

Greek perfection rather than Hebrew good.

His body reached a breaking point in hopes of getting his attention. Rather than consider and embrace his doubts and questions, Geoffrey assumed he must stop thinking about God altogether—a baby-with-the-bathwater approach. Only, that wasn't working either—his body continued to message him, which led him to get help through counseling.

If we only rely, however, on what we feel and experience regarding our faith, we are still not integrating our beliefs with our experience and attaching securely to God. We are not embodying our faith fully. We may love getting caught up in passionate worship services and soaring hymns but struggle to ground our faith in practices that stimulate our minds and balance our bodies. We sign up for the next conference, retreat, or seminar eager to find the secret that we assume we're missing, the secret that will help us sustain our wannabe-mystical experience on a daily basis.

Faith, thank God, is so much more than anything stored within any one part of us, including our brains. Integrated embodiment engages both our left and right hemispheres, our intellects, logic, and rational functioning as well as our imaginations, dreams, and creative impulses. Embodiment also requires embracing our bodies and all the trauma stored within us—from both past experiences and present dissonance between our beliefs and reality. The human soul includes the body.

Only as we learn to integrate our bodies within our spirituality can we become whole.

But before we explore practices toward this end (in chapter 11), we must begin by learning to pay attention to what our bodies are telling us.

Which is why it's essential to recognize the importance of finding ways to embody our faith. Thomas Keating explained:

> Most of us have a heavy burden of emotional junk accumulated from early childhood. The body serves as the storehouse for this undigested emotional material. The Spirit initiates the process of healing by evacuating the junk. This takes place as a result of the deep rest of mind and body in contemplative prayer.

The first step of contemplative prayer is growing in awareness and attunement. Learning to pay attention to our body and all that is going on both inside us and around us. Seeing how what we feel in our body relates to our environment, to relationships, events, and circumstances. Noticing how our bodies respond to what we see, hear, smell, taste, and touch.

Rather than viewing our bodies as the part of us we can't whip into shape or get under control, we must change how we think, feel, and see our bodies. Instead of despising our weight, our lust, our desires for things and other people, our choices we've made that were not in our best interests, we stop condemning and start investigating.

This shift is not simply attending to the symptoms manifested by our bodies by looking at the root causes of its distress, searching for the dissonance within us. If you truly want to close the gap between what you believe and what you experience, then your body is your crucial companion.

Why? Because it's the body—your nervous system shaped by a lifetime of experience—that cannot trust love.

Our body refuses to ignore what cannot be ignored. The body is our "truth teller," and the truth sets us free. We must practice being fully aware, mindful, in touch, synchronized with our body and its messages. When we let go of the often conditioned habit of holding our bodies at bay in contempt, of distancing ourselves from our bodies, then we discover how much it has to teach us.

As we begin to listen and learn from our body, we consider the possibility that just maybe we can trust love.

Restoring our soul requires reconnecting to our bodies.

**BLESSING**

*May you honor your body as a truth teller revealing*
*the divine in you.*
*May you know your body as a way to experience God.*
*May you be made whole—body, mind, soul, and will—*
*in the fullness of love.*

# 6

# TURNING

## DISCOVERING WE ARE BROKEN,
## BUT NOT BAD

*Where do we begin, the rubble or the sin?*

BASTILLE

I'll never forget the day Jesus met me in an adult bookstore.

Certainly not what I expected when I pulled into the parking lot. And I use the term *bookstore* loosely because it was basically a sad, decrepit storefront in a languishing strip mall at the edge of Denver. Books were in there somewhere, I suppose, but the place mostly featured porn magazines, DVDs, and assorted paraphernalia. Entering, I was assaulted by a pungent blend of industrial-strength ammonia mingled with a sickly sweet artificial fruit scent, both overlaying the smell of desperation.

In the back were video booths, which required quarter-coin tokens purchased from the sleepy, middle-aged man behind the register.

After wasting the few dollars I had on me, I felt a kind of frantic urgency. I was aware of the cycle of addiction and saddened that I was struggling to lose myself in the fantasy of this place—and now I was out of money. Credit or debit cards wouldn't work because they left a trail my wife could find. Feeling numb and hopeless, I wandered down the hall, selected another video booth, went in and locked the door, and got on my knees.

Not for the reason you might suspect or hope—not to pray. No, I knelt on the grimy, sticky floor and began groping along the dark corners in hopes of finding dropped quarters from previous customers. Anything to keep my chance at feeling seen, soothed, safe, and secure viable in this dead wonderland. Part of me wanted to go and part of me wanted to stay. *Just look at me*, I thought. *Dear God, who have I become?*

I found no coins that afternoon and instead left feeling far worse than when I entered. Gravity from the planet of shame quickly weighted every part of my body, leaving me heavy and torpid, struggling to catch my breath. As I drove away, the tears finally came until I began to detach from myself and bury my shame in order to resume my role as loving husband returning home to his beautiful young bride.

The next day I could not escape thoughts of that sordid place as I continued to see myself kneeling there in that video booth, scrounging for hope. Surrendering my heart before God was my only play to get through the day ahead, but I wasn't sure I could bear more shame. I began to pray anyway, silently, unable even to articulate all my thoughts and feelings.

A mental image rose up. There I was once again on the floor of that dark video booth, only I was not alone. Jesus was there, kneeling beside me, with his arm around my shoulders, pulling me into him.

"Of course you're here looking for comfort. Look at what happened to you. Look at all you've been through. Of course."

*Of course.*

## FIVE WS

That scene haunts me with the essence of grace.

It's the last thing I would expect to imagine or have pop into my mind. Jesus, there, in likely one of the worst moments of my life, kneeling alongside me, crying with me, holding me. Seeing me and looking into my heart and, instead of repugnance or condemnation, offering me compassion. Mercy. Comfort. Grace.

Nothing changed in my addictive behavior after this, not for a while still. But my understanding of what I had always considered my sinful nature, my dark heart, began to shift. Rather than the pathetic, weak, shameful coward I believed myself to be, I glimpsed how Jesus responded in a way that indicated my pain mattered.

So I began to wonder, what if my out-of-control behavior was not the product of my depravity but the result of my brokenness? What if the way I responded and mishandled my pain mattered, but not in the way I assumed? What if Jesus sees the brokenness beneath my behavior and loves me just the same as if I had been kneeling at the altar of a cathedral?

This radical notion began to change me deep inside.

It began to change the way I see God and see myself in relation to him.

I realized that until I understood that God loved me in my brokenness, I could not become whole. Through this process I have found it helpful to describe sin as what happens when we mishandle our brokenness, which is why I believe it essential that we understand the meaning of brokenness.

If you're still struggling with this shift, let's consider another likely basis for how you've defined your understanding of your struggles. Let's go back to when the original human struggle started, which wasn't long after God created the first humans.

Yes, I'm referring to Adam and Eve in the Garden of Eden and their big screw-up with the forbidden fruit—"the fall," as it's often referenced in theology, which in itself contributes to our misunderstanding and misperception.

The concept of the fall expresses a passive idea. An apple falls from a tree. A meteor falls from the sky. A chandelier falls from the ceiling. Framing the vulnerability of our humanity as "the fall" puts us in a position to view it as something ancient, mythic, symbolic—until we see how it happens to us now. Rather than some archaic belief that we either absorb or reactively reject, viewing what happened in the garden as "the turn" becomes not only more accurate but more hopeful.

Before you dismiss this shift to the turn as merely wishful thinking or a positive spin, just consider the difference it makes in how you see yourself, your flaws and failures, and your relationship to God. Simply ask yourself, *What was the nature of the turn as told in the book of Genesis? And how does this relate to my life today?*

One way to view the role of sin is to consider its inevitable impact. Imagine that you're very sick and in the ICU on life support and a ventilator. Without the medical devices and treatments, you will die from your illness. Nonetheless, you think you can get well on your own and decide to detach yourself from all the life-supporting gadgets. Have you ever noticed in so many movies the way a main character regains consciousness in a hospital emergency room and then immediately yanks out the IV, heart monitor, and any other tubes or wires connected to them? That's our human tendency—self-reliance, autonomy, independence.

Only, unlike our cinematic heroes, we don't last long without those machines to do what we simply cannot do for ourselves. Our sinful proclivity to go it on our own pulls the plug on the spiritual ventilator we need in order to keep breathing. When we choose autonomy and independence, we cut ourselves off from what's necessary for our survival and healing.

Death is not the punishment for our disobedience, for our sin. Paul tells us that the wages of sin is death (Romans 6:23), but death is the consequence of us pulling the plug. Death is what happens when you pull the plug on life support and get up and walk out of the hospital against doctor's orders. We pull the trigger for moving toward death, not God. Death is not the punishment for our sin, just the natural consequence of us disconnecting from the source of life.

Salvation, then, is getting plugged back in. Whoa.

Giving yourself—body, mind, emotions, and will—to trusting that inside the hospital you are safer and more secure than outside. Coming to your senses that in the care of the hospital you will be seen, soothed, safe, and secure. Securely attached to love, we not only restore our soul but also become whole.

To understand how and why we mishandle our brokenness, I find it helpful to think in five categories of our human condition, what I like to call the Five *W*s—wretchedness, weakness, woundedness, warfare, and wiring. Let's consider each of these in terms of how they shape our ability to attach to God.

## WRETCHEDNESS

"We all, like sheep, have gone astray, each of us has turned to our own way; and the LORD has laid on him the iniquity of us all" (Isaiah 53:6).

The word *wretch*, along with *wretched* and *wretchedness*, rarely gets used in everyday conversation. We hear it, though, every time we sing "Amazing Grace." You know, "Amazing grace, how sweet the sound that saved a wretch like me."

It's logical to assume wretch is just a synonym for sinner here, and one especially vile and wicked at that. This assumption used to make sense to me and fit the narrative of my life—of course I'm a wretch! But this assumption does not reflect the actual meaning of the word.

The origin of *wretch* likely comes from Anglo-Saxon and Old English usage of *wrecca*, meaning "banished or exiled." It referred to individuals forced to endure a nomadic existence, often due to poverty. They had no home, no family, nowhere to go. Charles

Dickens and other nineteenth-century authors used *wretch* to refer to what we might consider street people, the homeless, the panhandlers we see on street corners with cardboard signs asking for money for food.

So the status of being a wretch was due to poverty. And in biblical usage, poverty usually implies much more than economic status—it's essentially being poor in spirit. Thérèse of Lisieux considered our poverty to be our capacity for God. She believed that if you have no poverty, you have no capacity for him. When we sing about God's amazing grace that saved "a wretch like me," we're actually expressing that sense of being found after being lost, of being able to see after being blind. We were poor and exiled, wandering without a home—and God saved us because he loves us.

Being a wretch does not mean what you've probably assumed, just as I did.

Rather than a vile, pathetic, disgusting, unworthy fiend, you are simply homeless. A prodigal. A wanderer who's lost their way.

You are not bad—you are broken.

You are not disgusting and vile—you have been suffering alone.

You are not wicked and repulsive—you have been displaced in exile.

*Wretched* describes how you have been in exile from the arms of love.

Without the foundation of being seen, soothed, safe, and secure, you search and wander, assuming you're on your own. Or, in the words of another great hymn, "Come, Thou Fount of Every Blessing":

Prone to wander, Lord, I feel it,
Prone to leave the God I love;
Here's my heart, oh take and seal it;
Seal it for thy courts above.

Why would you wander from the God you love? Because you have not been seen, soothed, safe, and secure enough to trust him! Your embodied self has little to no reference point for trust. Remember, the Four *S*s are the basis for all trust.

## WEAKNESS

"'My grace is sufficient for you, for my power is made perfect in weakness.' . . . For when I am weak, then I am strong" (2 Corinthians 12:9-10).

Now that we understand the actual meaning of wretchedness, we can also understand our weakness more fully.

We all come into this world with unique gifts, skills, and abilities. We basically express who we are and assume on this basis we will be seen, soothed, safe, and secure. When we're not, we naturally draw conclusions for what we must do to survive. We take our vulnerabilities and limitations, often unconsciously, and hide them. We place our wounds and all those things we're ashamed of, all those dark thoughts and terrifying secrets, and segregate them from the rest of us. We bury them deep within or put them behind us, lock them up and throw away the key in hopes we can ignore them.

But we also create a major problem for ourselves when we do this: we set ourselves up for failure. If our deepest longing is to be known and loved, then we're hurting ourselves and creating a major obstacle to being known and loved. Because if we're only presenting our strengths, gifts, and abilities to others, we're taking ourselves—our full selves, including our weaknesses and failures—out of contention for being known and loved. We're creating a transactional system based on our performance.

Sure, we can be loved as long as we do what others want or what we want to get our needs met from them. We assume that if people really knew what we've done, where we've been, who we have been with, then they could never possibly love us. Rather than being open-handed and vulnerable in how we relate, we curate what we allow others to know and experience of us.

We relate to God the same way. Our performance mindset carries over so we perform and present who we think God wants us to be. We place ourselves on a treadmill of never good enough. So we run harder and faster, we get on a different treadmill, we do what we think we must in order to be acceptable. The irony, of course, is that our weaknesses —limitations and vulnerabilities, all the ways we've mishandled our pain—actually expand our capacity to be loved. By hiding them, we limit our ability to receive the love we so desperately crave.

If you want to experience being loved, you must bring all of you.

When I share about weakness, many respond with, "Oh, I know just what you mean. I'm weak and he is strong. I can do all things through Christ who strengthens me." Umm, no. But isn't that what Paul means in that passage from 2 Corinthians above? Not really.

The New Testament does teach us that God is our strength and that we can be strengthened by him. Paul does encourage us to embrace our weakness so that "Christ's power may rest on me" (2 Corinthians 12:9). And while Paul's context refers to his "thorn in my flesh" (2 Corinthians 12:7), the weakness to which I'm referring is more inherent and less circumstantial.

The weakness I'm interested in is our innate human limitation and vulnerability.

Weakness can be strengthened. But it must also be stewarded. We might know what it means to steward money or other gifts and resources. But what does it mean to steward weakness? And why should we consider our weakness a gift?

When we don't own our weakness, we set ourselves up for a vicious cycle. Think of it this way. You came into the world and you were helpless. Dependent. Vulnerable. With loving, attuned parents or caregivers, your vulnerability provides the natural opportunity for secure attachment, for bonding and being known.

The deepest desire of your heart is to be known—seen, soothed, safe, and secure. So when you deny yourself your weakness, you deny yourself of being human. When you hold back your vulnerability, you hold back being known for who you really are. You may succeed at being known, wanted, and loved for what you can do and whom you please. But you won't be satisfied because you lack the unconditional, limitless, "of course, of course" kind of love for which you were designed.

## WOUNDEDNESS

"For I am poor and needy, and my heart is wounded within me. I fade away like an evening shadow; I am shaken off like a locust" (Psalm 109:22-23).

Our wounds fit into one or more categories based on how well we were seen and soothed, how safe and secure we felt, and the conclusions and strategies we formed based on what we did and did not get. We have wounds of presence and wounds of absence. Wounds of presence are things done to us that never should have happened, while wounds of absence are things that should have happened that went undone.

Most of us have experienced both, although wounds of presence tend to be easier to recognize. Wounds of absence may not be recognized until years or even decades later when someone realizes the extent of their unmet needs during childhood. In my counseling work, I encounter people who are acutely aware of their wounds, which is often why they seek my help. Others, however, may have symptomatic or problematic behaviors or emotions without being aware of any wounding.

The reality is that many people did have a childhood without overt wounds of presence. But none of us gets through life without some wounds, and wounds of absence can be tricky. People often become aware of their impact before they recognize the actual wounds themselves. Many times our survival strategies are so well constructed that we don't realize the default defenses we have in place.

Even Jesus experienced both kinds of wounds during his time living as a human. When we think about Jesus being wounded, the first place our minds may go is to his physical torture on the cross. But Jesus experienced other wounds throughout his life. People who knew him rejected him, mocked him, taunted him. He was misunderstood and treated with contempt. He was tempted by the devil. Even his disciples, the individuals who knew him best and loved him most, betrayed and abandoned him. Jesus was wounded throughout his life.

Regardless of the kinds of wounds we experienced, the hurt was traumatic. Perhaps we didn't get what we needed, what every child deserves, and suffered as a result. We experienced things as a kid, a teen, an adult that no one should have to endure. Therapists distinguish between "small t" and "large T" traumas. The large traumas are usually self-evident—events, experiences, incidents, relationships that irrefutably hurt us. The smaller traumas are what we experience chronically just from the offenses of others, the losses and pain that often feel greater because they remind us of our Traumas.

Richard Rohr says that unless pain is transformed, pain is transmitted to those around us because our wretchedness, weakness, and woundedness often leave us looking for ways to escape our pain and find comfort. This makes us particularly vulnerable for the enemy of our souls to exploit our weakness.

## WARFARE

"Then I heard a loud voice in heaven saying, 'Now God's salvation has come! Now God has shown his power as King! Now his Messiah has shown his authority! For the one who stood before our God and accused believers day and night has been thrown out of heaven'" (Revelation 12:10 GNT).

Like the way "sin" is often viewed, absorbed, and enacted, the idea of evil and spiritual warfare tends to skew as well. Simply put, I fear it tilts toward the extremes—either a dismissive, superstitious, uneducated view of unfortunate events in the world or a terrified, concealed-carry-cross mindset ready to shake every bush for the demon lurking. I have a more-than-healthy respect for evil, for the devil, and the necessity of spiritual warfare. In my own journey of healing and in my ministry, I have encountered evil. And so I have a more-than-healthy respect for its scope, stealth, and power. But I also believe, as C. S. Lewis so brilliantly depicts in *The Screwtape Letters*, that the enemy of our souls can operate with subtlety, with misdirection and distraction.

When you consider warfare, you may think of demonic deliverance and demonstrative preachers, but I believe we experience warfare as an aspect of our brokenness primarily through deception and lies. Lies about who we are and who God is, deception about how our needs will or will not be met.

We have an accuser who is hurling insults at us day and night (Revelation 12:10). Our unsurrendered weakness and unhealed woundedness become the landing pad for warfare and the launching pad for the wretchedness of self-exile from love.

The war is against what is true about us.

What's true about us is that we are fearfully and wonderfully made, beautifully and gloriously made in the image of God—and that we are vulnerable and dependent. When we remain ignorant of these truths or lose sight of them, then the enemy works to convince us of two essential lies: (1) You can't trust God because he's not good; and (2) You can do a better job of being God and providing what you need—because you can't trust him or his love.

Summed up, these lies come down to "Love does not have you," therefore "Get what you can get on your own right now." In order to engage with warfare, we must confront the lies and accusations, expose the deception, and pour truth over the flames of gaslighting. Even after you identify the lies stuck in your mind, you may continue struggling with their impact. Which is why you must focus on what's true as you recognize them.

Here are some of the common lies and accusations the enemy uses—along with what is true:

Lie: No one can love you after all that you've done—you're too damaged, too messed up.

Truth: Nothing can separate you from the love of God. We are all broken and need love.

Lie: If your family found out about your secret, they would hate you and abandon you.

Truth: Admitting your brokenness sets you free, no matter how others respond.

Lie: Your worth depends on your appearance, your luxury items, and your dollar signs.

Truth: Your worth is secure because God made you and loves you just as you are.

Lie: You are too much and others cannot handle all that you're carrying.

Truth: You can be seen, soothed, safe, and secure by others willing to risk loving you.

You can be securely attached to God who says you are not too much—you're just right.

## WIRING

"I praise you because I am fearfully and wonderfully made; your works are wonderful, I know that full well" (Psalm 139:14).

Frequently, the men and women I counsel describe thought patterns, choices, habits, patterns, and addictions that transcend their ability to understand themselves, let alone control or stop these recurrent intrusions. I think about the many men who feel compelled to act out in ways that appall, terrify, thrill, and torture them.

I recall the women who feel paralyzed by ambivalence, unable to leave an unhealthy, even abusive, relationship yet knowing that they are surely in danger emotionally, sexually, mentally, and perhaps physically because of their willingness to remain with their spouse or partner.

In the previous chapter, we explored embodiment. One of the most important aspects of embodiment is focusing on our central nervous systems and the miles of neural pathways within our bodies. All of our early life experiences and what we experience every day shape these neural pathways in our brain. The degree to which we experienced being seen, soothed, safe, and secure remains embedded in our neural networks and neurons in our wiring.

By wiring I simply mean our neural networks. Our genetics and other variables make up our wiring. The ways we move through life with our vulnerabilities and limitations also shape our wiring. Our weaknesses and how we steward them affect our wiring. Our genetics and biological variables contribute to our wiring.

Here's the good news, though: While our wiring plays an essential role in who we are and how we close the gap between belief and experience, our neural paths can be rewired. We can learn practices that literally change the way we think and feel. We can adopt practices (which we will explore in chapter 11) that literally change the way we think and feel. As Curt Thompson explains:

> Our attachment patterns, translated into and through our neural networks, not only affect our relationships with other people, they are one of the primary forces shaping our relationship with God. Whatever our dominant patterns tend to be, we will relate with and assume things about God through those same neural

networks. (After all, he created our brains and doesn't bypass them when he invites us to a personal encounter with him.)

Shifting our understanding of brokenness requires us to honor our embodiment, the fact that our wiring impacts what we think, what we feel, and how we relate to God and others. We must realize the intricacy and beauty of how our brains function. If we are indeed wonderfully and fearfully made as the psalmist observes, then we need help untangling connections made in our brains that no longer protect or serve us.

**Table 6.1.** The interrelationship of the five *W*s and the four *S*s: you are not bad, you are broken

| | How You Recognize It | How It Impacts the Four *S*s | How It Impedes Secure Attachment | How It Can Become a Bridge to Secure Attachment |
|---|---|---|---|---|
| **1** Wretch-edness | Impoverished, homeless, exiled, poor in spirit | Distrusts others and God to meet needs | Reinforces doubt that love and security are possible | Compels you to find security in the love of God and others |
| **2** Wound-edness | Hurts and harm at the hands of others | Reinforces belief that needs will never be met | Trauma goes unaddressed and unpro-cessed | Pulls you toward divine love for healing and the care of others |
| **3** Weakness | Human limitations and vulner-ability, powerlessness | Facilitates a victim mindset or need for control | Tilts toward extremes of hopelessness or complete self-reliance | Invites you to surrender to the strength and power of love |
| **4** Warfare | Accusations and deception leading to lies we believe | Leaves you vulnerable to believing enemy's lies | Prone to distrust God and rely on yourself | Requires focusing on what is true and relying on the power of love |
| **5** Wiring | The physical self: specifi-cally, our central nervous system composed of countless neural networks | Creates default neural pathways based on early conditioning | Prevents secure attachment because of those neural networks | Focusing on truth and practicing embodied spirituality rewires neural pathways |

## OF COURSE . . . OF COURSE

So now what? What difference does understanding these Five *W*s make?

Like the Four *S*s (seen, soothed, safe, and secure), understanding our Five *W*s makes an enormous difference. As we begin reconsidering old assumptions and false beliefs, we allow ourselves to question and consider that we've been deceived and misled about what is true about us and about God.

We realize that our wretchedness results from insecure attachment and the lie that God is not trustworthy.

We consider our weakness and we own it. As opposed to burying or hiding it, we steward it and view it as the gift it really is.

As we own our weakness and tell the story to others, we entrust our woundedness. As we trust and receive, our brokenness gradually starts to heal. We discover we can somehow be sustained and held until a future time of wholeness. What the Bible calls sin is the result of how our Five *W*s come together and intersect in our lives.

Just consider the difference when we view brokenness as the result of how these Five *W*s collide:

An addiction to food and overeating is gluttonous . . . and results from an allergy in the body, from childhood trauma and conditioning, from false messages accepted into thought patterns.

Adultery is immoral . . . and results from loneliness, insecurity, sexualized thoughts, past sexual abuse, fear of intimacy, and believing the incomplete narrative formed by a spouse's inability to meet all needs.

Worshiping success through the accumulation of money, luxuries, Rolex watches, Louis Vuitton bags, enviable vacations, and social media followers is idolatrous . . . and results from deprivation, neglect, fear of failure, fear of success, insecurity, self-loathing, poor body image, compensation, and cultural conditioning.

Fill in the blank with whatever your favorite sins might be.

Rather than stick with the old binary way of viewing them as right and wrong, black and white, the contextual shades of gray reveal much more about who you are, why you struggle, and how much God loves you and wants to meet you in the shadows. Yes, these behaviors can be wrong and sinful, but the Five *W*s explain why they are not who you are ultimately according to God. Rather than sticking with the assumption that if God is inherently good, then I must be inherently bad, what if you considered the possibility that God won't let you go?

What if you filled in the blank with your most shameful sins and heard God say, "Of course . . . of course you're afraid and insecure and eating that entire carton of Rocky Road"?

Or "Of course . . . of course you're hooking up to escape the pain of loneliness and stress you're under . . . of course."

Or "Of course . . . you're shopping online and buying another pair of shoes, another outfit, more jewelry because you feel so ashamed of your body, your weight, your wrinkles."

*Of course* . . .

This reflects one of my favorite quotes from the Ambrosian rites of the Catholic Mass when the priest sings to God, "You bent down over our wounds and healed us, giving us medicine stronger than our afflictions, a mercy greater than our fault. In this way even sin, by virtue of your invincible love, served to elevate us to the divine life."

Because out of our need, out of the brokenness we glimpse within our own Five *W*s, we discover a capacity and longing for love we tend to overlook. To dismiss. To assume cannot exist—or at least exist for us.

What if everything you have been taught and believe about sin is not simply wrong but hindering your relationship with God?

Preventing you from experiencing the divine compassion, kindness, gentleness, and patience you long for?

Impeding the healing you have within reach?

Sin can stand in our way to knowing God. But often the bigger problem is our focus on our sin and getting stuck there. When we're stuck, we struggle to close the gap between what we believe and what we experience.

But only when we courageously begin to accept and own the experiences leading to our delta can we begin to see what was once a gap becomes two rivers running together.

Pain and brokenness of the delta is where the river and the sea of love become one.

In order to fully experience the riches of grace, we must confront our impoverished condition. We must look at the damage we've caused in the lives of others to grasp what forgiveness is all about—to understand why God forgives us. There's no good reason . . . other than love.

You can continue to view God as holy and perfect and his sovereignty as what matters most. Or you can realize that sovereignty is heightened when it humbles itself to love those who are beloved—having limitless and infinite power, and letting it all go . . . to cry as a baby in a chilly stable reeking of manure. Incarnational love.

You are deeply known and deeply loved.

Yes, you are broken and you are prone to mishandle your pain.

But even at your worst, your attachment to God is secure.

Your brokenness is your *bridge*—not your barrier—to experiencing God.

His *love* has you.

His love has *always* had you.

His love will always have *you*.

## BLESSING

*May your heart and mind be open*
*to understanding brokenness.*
*May you have fresh insight into the ways you have*
*mishandled your pain.*
*May you know that your brokenness creates a bridge*
*to experiencing God.*
*May you awaken to a new awareness of God's presence.*

# 7

# WHOLLY

## BECOMING WHOLE AND HOLY

*What we are all more or less lacking at this moment*
*is a new definition of holiness.*

PIERRE TEILHARD DE CHARDIN

Recently while leading a retreat for a group of pastors, I asked them which passage in Scripture best illustrates the holiness of God. One immediately responded, "Isaiah 6!" and then proceeded to quote the first three verses which describe God seated on a throne high and exalted as angelic seraphim proclaim, "Holy, holy, holy is the LORD Almighty; the whole earth is full of his glory" (Isaiah 6:3). Most of the group nodded their assent for this illustrious passage.

"Others that come to mind?" I prompted.

"Moses encountering the burning bush? He had to take off his sandals and could not look upon God's face." More nodding of agreement.

After a few seconds someone else said, "Well, there's also that Old Testament scene—in Samuel or Chronicles, I think—where the Israelites are moving the Ark of the Covenant. The oxen stumbled and the Ark began to fall, so Uzzah reached out to steady it. God was so angry that he touched the Ark, though, that he struck him dead."

"Right—has that scene ever troubled you?" I said. "It emphasizes the distinction between God's holiness and our sinfulness similar to what we see in Isaiah 6. You'll recall that an angel used tongs to lift a burning coal from the altar and then touched Isaiah's lips, which atoned for his sins and removed his guilt."

A few members of the group looked down as the room fell silent.

"Those are both powerful illustrations," I said, "but I believe the scene in the Bible best illustrating God's holiness is found in John 8—so let's take a look."

"Isn't that where the woman caught in adultery is brought before Jesus?"

"Yes, it is." I smiled and then read through that very scene before making my case.

Dragged from a bedroom by the local religious leaders and brought before Jesus, this woman faced shame that should have been lethal. According to the Law of Moses, she should be stoned to death. Her accusers viewed her plight as a perfect way to trap Jesus, whose message of grace and forgiveness went against the legalism they had placed at the very foundation of their faith. Only Christ turned the tables on those judging and condemning her.

"Where are your accusers?" Jesus asked the surely traumatized woman dragged before him by zealous, letter-of-the-law leaders. "Didn't even one of them condemn you?" This after Jesus had answered the legalists' question about whether the woman should be stoned, as prescribed by the Law of Moses, by stooping and scrawling something on the dusty ground. "Sure," he told them, "you can stone her. But only the one who has never sinned gets to throw those stones." Once again, he bent down and wrote on the ground, even as the accusers walked away. The woman said to Jesus, "No, Lord. No one condemns me now," to which he added, "Neither do I. Go and sin no more" (John 8:1-11, my paraphrase).

Surely the wounds of this woman weighed on her. Presumably naked and cowering there before the local authorities, she feared for her life. Or perhaps she preferred imminent death over the shame and humiliation, the sense of being used and perhaps violated, of being judged and treated as less than human by the religious establishment's leaders. Whatever she may have expected, I doubt she anticipated the way Jesus regarded her.

Jesus saw her wounds and offered soothing and a sense of safety and security beyond any she had ever known. His heart was there to introduce her to a different way of living. He did not condemn her because he had a vision for her, seeing beneath the act for which she was brought before him. He disarms her accusers by drawing in the dirt, redirecting their attention to their own vulnerabilities and indiscretions.

Simply put, Jesus viewed her as holy.

## SPIRITUAL GRAVITY

You may be wondering the same thing many of those pastors did: How exactly does this scene illustrate God's holiness? Especially in light of those Old Testament passages, which seem more direct and clear-cut?

It's a fair question when considering what we've been told: God's perfect holiness prevents us, imperfect and unholy, from drawing closer to him. He cannot look on our sinful, wretched condition unless there's some kind of filter, buffer, or atonement. Although Christ provided that atonement, we still experience this separation in the gap between our beliefs and our lives. So we work hard to be good enough to deserve God's love and to earn enough grace for our latest transgression.

Sound familiar? So many of us relate to God in this way, forcing ourselves into a narrative that seems far removed from the reality of our lives, widening that gap between what we believe and what we actually experience. In pursuit of divine connection, we experience greater distance from God.

A key contributor to this gulf is our skewed view of holiness. God's holiness is moral perfection, and we are morally imperfect. God is inherently holy, and we clearly are not holy.

But what if our understanding of holiness is not only inaccurate but coloring our entire perspective on who we are and who God is?

So often, we're conditioned to view the holiness of God as an ideal, something unattainable that distances us from God. This ideal of holiness leaves us with a high degree of pressure and a low degree of joy.

In order to understand the holiness of God, we must stop viewing holiness as this unattainable commodity distancing us from God and begin realizing what it means in the context of how we relate to Jesus. The reason I say this—and why I chose that scene in John 8—may have more to do with physics than theology.

Why physics? Because holiness as we have learned it places God at the center of everything, perfect and powerful beyond anything we can fully fathom. So rather than the burning bush Moses encountered, God might be more like the way we think about our sun. If we stare at it directly, we go blind from the pure-white intensity of its light. If we get too close, we combust and burn up. So we accept that we can never draw close to the sun—or the holiness of God—because it will destroy us. The best we can do is ceaselessly strive to get to the point where we're as close as an unholy human can be, which leaves us trapped by centrifugal force.

As I understand centrifugal force in its simplest form, it's the way something moving in a circular motion tries to push away from the center of that circle. I think about one of my favorite amusement park rides when I was a kid called the Rotor. You would go into what seemed to be this big circular room and stand with your back against the wall. Strapped in almost elbow-to-elbow with other riders, you then felt the circular walls begin to move slowly clockwise, picking up speed faster and faster until finally the floor dropped out from under your feet, leaving you hanging on the wall, stuck there by centrifugal force!

Or consider the way your washing machine leaves your clothes stuck to its outer edges after the spin cycle. As they spin around and around faster and faster, centrifugal force pushes them away from the center of the metal drum. You probably have other examples that come to mind.

The best example of centrifugal force in your life, however, may have gone unnoticed. It's the way you try to work harder to get closer to God, spinning in your own energy but never seeming to get nearer to him the way you long to know him. The harder you try, the more you feel like you can never do enough, pray enough, study the Bible enough, or resist temptation enough.

So what happens if you stop spinning in place with centrifugal spirituality?

You allow gravity to pull you.

Gravitational force occurs when we're pulled toward something of greater mass and density. The earth's gravity keeps our feet on the ground and causes things we drop to fall to its surface. Based on physics, every object in the universe is pulling on every other object because of gravitational force. They are trying to get closer, to come together.

So rather than spinning in place because we're separated from God's holiness, what if God's holiness is the center of spiritual gravity pulling us closer? What if we stop striving and surrender to his love?

The Bible tells us that we have eternity in our hearts (Ecclesiastes 3:11), that we are created in God's image (Genesis 1:27). Jesus said, "And when I am lifted up from the earth, I will draw everyone to myself" (John 12:32 NLT). Rather than being repulsed and repelled by the sin of the woman caught in adultery, Jesus moved toward her, offering her forgiveness and grace instead of condemnation and punishment. She experienced secure attachment to God in a way that was impossible under the Law of Moses as administered by the religious leaders who caught her in the midst of her immorality.

Instead, she surrendered to the gravitational pull of God's love.

In recent years, though, I've reconsidered and discovered my understanding of holiness is not the barrier to knowing God I'd assumed. It actually invites me to draw closer to him. I came to this conclusion recently after reading several popular books about holiness.

They tended to fall into two camps. One took a fairly traditional approach and politely shamed readers for no longer aspiring to holiness as a priority in their faith. This viewpoint reinforces the perfect and absolute holiness of God and the utter depravity and permanent sin stain in human beings. The other books shot down that viewpoint by proceeding to deconstruct the theological notion of holiness and redefine it as a kind of universal goodness, a benign, tepid awareness of positivity.

Both sides of this spectrum seem to miss the point. Neither seems connected to my real-life experiences or those of faith pilgrims whom I admire. Which sent me exploring what holiness is actually all about—the life-giving pull of love toward union with God. What I found is perhaps summed up best by Eugene Peterson's rendering of this passage from Paul's letter to the Ephesians:

How blessed is God! And what a blessing he is! He's the Father of our Master, Jesus Christ, and takes us to the high places of blessing in him. Long before he laid down earth's foundations, he had us in mind, had settled on us as *the focus of his love, to be made whole and holy by his love.* Long, long ago he decided to adopt us into his family through Jesus Christ. (What pleasure he took in planning this!) He wanted us to enter into the celebration of his lavish gift-giving by the hand of his beloved Son. (Ephesians 1:3-6 MSG, my emphasis)

Throughout the Bible the message is the same as we see here: if we want to know holiness, we must know Jesus.

Just as our view of God is often inaccurately biased, our perception of Jesus may also need adjustment. He is not the flannel-graph Sunday school Jesus waiting to bust us because we can't be as passively perfect as he is. Recently I was in a consignment shop that sold vintage and antique items when I looked up and saw one of those church-wall pictures of Jesus—only a cartoon bubble had been added: "I'm watching you—Thou Shalt Not Steal!"

Yet this is not the Jesus we see in the Gospels.

His holiness is not about getting the rules right or fulfilling religious expectations. He makes it clear that understanding the holiness of God requires shifting our focus from a legalistic, centrifugal focus to the loving, gravitational pull of an intimate, secure relationship with the God who looks like Jesus. This shift in no way diminishes the perfect pureness and sinless supremacy of who God is but instead reveals who he is on his terms. Because when God sent Jesus to live as both God and man, he revealed how he wants to be known—as a person who loves us with life, grace, and mercy.

Not everyone liked shifting their view of God and his holiness based on what Jesus taught. When Jesus healed a lame man on the Sabbath, the Jewish religious leaders pounced on what they perceived as this huge sacrilege, compounded because Jesus called God his own Father, making himself God's equal (John 5:16-18).

Why didn't Jesus condemn sinners and follow the rules like they did? How could they consider him the Messiah with such blatant disregard for religious rules and Pharisaic protocol? Who did he think he was? Because the Son of God would not behave so contrary to their own standards and expectations.

The kind of holiness Jesus displayed during his life on earth seems a lot, well, earthier. More human. More grounded and humble. Less ethereal and separate. More restorative and grace-based. Less restrictive and merit-based. Even when looking at Jesus, some of us still carry baggage about the person of Jesus.

Because when you consider who Jesus had a problem with during his time on earth, it's the legalists, the chess players, the Pharisees who focused on external behavior rather than internal spiritual posture. With sinners, including the very worst offenders—thieves, con men, prostitutes, and corrupt tax collectors—Jesus withheld condemnation and instead offered grace, compassion, and forgiveness.

Rather than condemn and punish the woman caught in adultery, Jesus stood up to her accusers and offered her grace. He showed her a different kind of holiness. A holiness that was first and foremost relational and gravitational, pulling her toward his grace rather than away from God as defined by the Law.

When Jesus told this woman to go and sin no more, was he assuming she had the ability to choose never to sin again? I don't think so, not if we define our condition as the permanent blight separating us from God's holiness. By that definition, we don't have a choice—we're "inherently sinful" simply by being born human. So if that's not what Jesus intended, what did he mean when he told her to go and sin no more?

What if "go and sin no more" might be more accurately understood as "be restored and no longer broken"?

As I see it, holiness is all about wholeness and best viewed by reflecting on the divine love revealed in the person of Jesus.

It's about a new way of living and relating to God anchored by the reality that we are seen, soothed, safe, and secure.

Holiness invites us to live in union with the God who looks just like Jesus.

Right now you might be uncomfortable with how we're describing holiness here—perhaps it seems too human, which therefore diminishes the divine. Understood.

But just consider for a moment how your relationship with God changes if holiness is about wholeness rather than perfection.

## COME AND GET YOUR LOVE

You will recall that I prefer the term *turning* when describing what happened in the Garden of Eden with Adam and Eve. Falling implies a breach, a lowering, a distance, a separation from the higher place from which you fell to the lower ground where you landed. Turning, by comparison, indicates this change of direction, which, as C. S. Lewis points out, is either drawing us closer to or away from God, others, and ourselves:

> Every time you make a choice you are turning the central part of you, the part of you that chooses, into something a little different than it was before. And taking your life as a whole, with all your innumerable choices, all your life long you are slowly turning this central thing into a heavenly creature or a hellish creature: either into a creature that is in harmony with God, and with other creatures, and with itself, or else into one that is in a state of war and hatred with God, and with its fellow creatures, and with itself.

These words may land hard with you—the reality that everything you do reflects that you're either moving toward God or away from him. But your choices determine your direction. You may view your decisions as matters of choosing to rebel against or to obey God, but this view falls prey to its own inherent self-limitation. As Yogi Berra might put it, how can we stop screwing up when we can't stop screwing up?

The other view—of sin, as choosing to move toward or away from relationship with God, with other people, and with ourselves —reflects the restored dignity and redeemed story we have because of who Jesus is. The problem, though, is that by misunderstanding holiness, we also fail to grasp who Jesus is within a personal context. Yes, he is our Lord and Savior, the Son of God, our mediator before the Father, the Messiah, Prince of Peace, and Alpha and Omega. But that's not all of who Jesus is—he is also relational, present, and personal.

If we don't have a fresh understanding of holiness, we will remain seemingly separate and detached from God. The irony is that we can't actually move away from God. Wherever we go, he is there. Even in adult bookstores or hotel rooms with prostitutes. Even when shopping online for items you don't need and can't afford. When hiding empty wine bottles.

This fresh understanding of holiness is the essence of the gospel. God invites us in and shares his holiness with us. The holiness of Peter letting Jesus wash his feet. The holiness of an unexpected conversation between Jesus and a Samaritan woman at a well.

Holiness is how God sees you, feels about you, thinks about you, and acts toward you. Holiness motivates God to extend his love in every way to us. This is why God is the perfect parent and why, when we are in union with him, we are seen, soothed, safe, and secure.

This divine secure attachment transcends even the best parental love. And once we experience this secure attachment, we abide in this loving relationship. No longer stuck in the gap, we grow and mature. Jesus made it explicitly clear that the way to know him and know the Father is by abiding and growing: "As the Father has loved me, so have I loved you. Now remain in my love" (John 15:9).

God the Father loves you as much as Jesus.

You may or may not believe that right now. But whether you consider yourself full of faith or lacking faith, whether straight or LGBTQ+, Calvinist or Arminian, or someone who defies labels and reflects the often-contradictory idiosyncrasies of humanity, God the Father loves you as much as Jesus.

"As the Father has loved me, so have I loved you. Now remain in my love."

Right now, you have all the love you long for, need, want, crave, and desire. If you don't believe me, keep reading.

Love motivates God to extend his holiness to us through his Son and through his Spirit. He is not separated from us but chooses to dwell with us and in us. Rather than the distance I felt growing up whenever I heard "Holy, Holy, Holy," I now like to imagine Jesus singing Redbone's '70s classic "Come and Get Your Love." Because his love is right there, right in front of us for the taking and experiencing and sharing. His holiness draws us closer rather than pushing us away.

Come and get your love, come and get your love, come and get your love now.

This is why we must learn to rethink our understanding of holiness.

Come and get your love, come and get your love, come and get your love now.

Because attaching securely to Christ means knowing that love has you like nothing else ever has or ever will. Beginning to know this love as embodied experience, you are spiritually grafted to God in a way that has nothing to do with your performance or faithfulness.

Experiencing this love, you are spiritually sustained and linked to God, like a tree branch to a trunk, in a way that you cannot accomplish on your own. This is the essence of healthy, secure attachment, the kind that allows you to trust in the One who loves you most and loves you best. This is what it means to "be perfect, therefore, as your heavenly Father is perfect" (Matthew 5:48).

Perfection is wholeness.

So come and get your love.

## COEXISTING AND CONTRADICTING

Now I'm aware that you may struggle with viewing perfection as wholeness. After all, perfect is a loaded word. But it's time to unload some of that baggage getting in the way of how you view holiness.

Perfect in the way Jesus instructs us to be perfect sounds a lot like unattainable holiness—great to strive for but always beyond reach. If that's the case, then why would Jesus deliberately set us up for frustrating failure? He, perhaps better than anyone, knows we are not perfect, which is why he came to make us whole and invite us to live in union with him.

Which leads us back to recalling that Hebrew good is better than Greek perfect. Instead of perfect, we might translate what Jesus said here as whole—"be *whole*, therefore, as your heavenly Father is *complete*."

Wholeness is the key to understanding holiness.

Because wholeness is the essence of holiness.

As broken human beings we experience wholeness as learning to accept all different parts of ourselves and allow them to coexist. God, who is utterly and totally whole and complete in three persons, models this for us through the Trinity. All three are essential parts of who God is and are the essence of who God is. It's because of his example and essence that we discover that all of our parts are welcome, especially the broken parts.

Holiness—pure, life-giving, relational wholeness—invites our often disparate, sometimes contradictory parts and pieces to be transformed into a new wholeness. This is how the God that looks like Jesus restores our souls.

The truth of this transformation is illustrated by one of my favorite art forms—*kintsugi*. This ancient Japanese technique restores broken pieces of pottery back together by mending edges with precious metal powder, usually gold or silver. The result transforms a useless piece that would likely be thrown away into a new, one-of-a-kind ceramic vessel veined with precious metal. The restored pottery becomes beautiful and more valuable after being broken than before. Kintsugi exemplifies the Japanese aesthetic sensibility known as *wabi-sabi*, finding beauty in imperfection.

Kintsugi makers do not hide the fractures or the past; they mend it to make it new.

This is holiness.

Holiness hides nothing. Discards nothing.

Holiness is the energy of God making all things whole. Or wholly new.

This is why I actually have a stunning kintsugi bowl on display in my counseling office to show to clients. There's just something so powerful about running your fingers along the cracks and edges, tracing jagged golden streaks that resemble borders around tiny countries. Kintsugi offers a tangible metaphor for embracing one's flaws and failures, indiscretions and imperfections.

"Like clay in the hand of the potter, so are you in my hand," God told the people of Israel (Jeremiah 18:6). But even after our vessels are chipped and cracked, broken and shattered, God restores us into something more and better than before. We become his handiwork, his *poiēma*, his workmanship, his kintsugi. God's holiness, like the precious gold and silver in kintsugi, unites our broken pieces into a new wholeness.

So rather than suppressing, hiding, condemning, shaming, and numbing the parts of our stories we don't like or want to include, we discover how they become raw material for a new creation. This is the Jesus way.

Accurately understanding God's holiness allows room and gives us permission to welcome or reclaim disowned parts and broken pieces. To see them integrated into wholeness that creates something more beautiful than we imagined possible. Our union with the divine restores us to wholeness, to the man or woman God created and designed us to be.

It's as if he's saying, "All the fractured pieces no longer exist as shards. I am bringing the precious pieces together, bonded with gold and made into something whole and new."

Holiness is not a static state of being but a dynamic process. The process of becoming holy, like God is holy and intends for us to be holy, requires action, movement, growth, that long obedience in the same direction, as Eugene Peterson described discipleship.

Holiness unites you with God.

Wholeness invites you to surrender the shards and broken pieces of your life.

Together, they dare you to discover that you are better broken.

After all, it's the broken parts of you that most need to be seen, soothed, safe, and secure.

It's your brokenness that becomes whole in union with God's love.

It's your brokenness that becomes holy in union with God's love.

## BLESSING

*May you see God's holiness in the humility*
*and humanity of Jesus.*
*May your brokenness create space*
*to experience God's holiness.*
*May your union with the holiness of love align you*
*with wholeness.*

# 8

# KNOWN

## FACING OUR DEEPEST DESIRE
## AND GREATEST FEAR

*Love takes off the masks that we fear we cannot live without
and know we cannot live within.*

JAMES BALDWIN

When I first began sharing my story of recovery and healing from trauma, abuse, and addiction, the shame I experienced often felt overwhelming. Not only was I standing up in front of people to talk about taboo topics such as abuse, addiction, and infidelity, but I was revealing that these were all intimate parts of me, my story, the man standing before them in real time. No surprise then that getting to the point where I stood before large audiences did not happen overnight.

The more practice I had telling my story, however, the easier it flowed. Shame began to dissipate as I leaned into the courage to reveal how God used my brokenness to build something authentic and holy. Being known for who I am, not who I used to believe I was, became healing in itself. As the size of my audiences grew, I also felt less vulnerable.

Sure, I was talking about some of the most horrific moments of my life, but I wasn't staring into the faces of a dozen people looking intently back at me. I was a speaker in front of hundreds and then thousands, which created a kind of distance, both emotionally and physically. When I finally shared at a large event before more than a couple thousand participants, I celebrated that afterward I felt virtually no shame hangover at all.

A few days later, however, being exposed for a different reason sent me reeling.

Talking with a close friend, Peter, I took a risk. One that resulted in saturating me with shame in ways I hadn't experienced. I asked my friend for some financial advice, for his recommendations on how to invest wisely for maximum return. He was happy to help and began to ask questions, which included specifics about my income, savings, and debt amounts.

"And what about credit card debt?" Peter asked.

In the few seconds it took me to answer, I had that feeling you may have experienced before. The one where you're paying at the grocery store or finishing your meal in a restaurant only to hear someone, a cashier or waiter, say, "I'm sorry but your card has been declined. Is there another one you'd like me to try?" Now imagine that sense of shame on steroids, magnified by the Hubble Space Telescope and broadcast throughout an Olympic stadium filled with a hundred thousand people all gasping at once.

As I said the number aloud, I stared into my friend's eyes, fully anticipating the shock, horror, and contempt he felt at my irresponsibility. Successful, responsible adults simply did not allow themselves to carry that kind of consumer credit debt, did they? And yet there I was, as emotionally naked and ashamed as I could be without a fig leaf in sight.

I could stand in front of thousands and let them know me as a sex addict.

But I couldn't bear for this friend to know the shame contained by this number.

I wanted his help, but the cost seemed too great.

No one is exempt from such moments, and you may feel the blood rush to your cheeks right now as you recall your own moment of shameful revelation. We all have them. Perhaps yours has to do with your weight, a certain physical feature, a moral failure no one knows about, a secret addiction still hidden in the dark.

A client I once worked with shared with me that he's often posted pictures and videos of himself on hook-up apps and sites, but that he doesn't like his wife to see him naked. He's willing to send the most intimate images of his body anonymously to strangers but struggles to reveal himself to the person he loves most. This paradox frustrates and confuses him, leaving him feeling stuck in the desire to be known without risking rejection.

This dilemma also manifests in less obvious ways. In college my roommate, a focused and highly motivated business major, budgeted his time each day to make sure all assignments were completed to the best of his ability and on time. He would take his course syllabus on the first day of class and start working on big assignments and comprehensive research papers right away—yes, he was that guy.

I, on the other hand, usually lost my course syllabus before midterms and barely kept up with the assigned reading. And when it came to essays and research papers, I brewed a pot of coffee and pushed through an all-nighter. Watching me basically do the opposite of his meticulous method, my roommate came to resent me. Because sometimes I made a better grade.

The differences in our approach amused me until one day years later when a counselor asked me why I chose to work that way. Yes, I obviously did well under pressure, she observed, but what was the payoff I received for setting myself up to work this way? Although I'd never considered it before, instantly I knew. *I didn't have to risk revealing my true self or my actual abilities.* By always waiting to the last minute, I had an automatic excuse. If I performed poorly, I didn't let it bother me because I hadn't really tried. And if I received a high grade or validation, then I could feel good about not risking more effort than required.

Your hide-and-seek style of being known may come out at the office. You work harder than anyone on your team but dodge taking the credit because someday you might have to take the blame. Or it could be as simple as working hard to create an image of success to compensate for the crippling insecurity lurking beneath your luxury-brand clothing and designer sunglasses.

We all want to be known and valued, but if we can minimize the risk of rejection or come up with a way to explain away others' indifference, then we hedge our bets. Because when we reveal ourselves and are not seen, valued, and known, the wound to our soul gushes with shame.

## HOW SHAME TAKES ROOT

Learning to experience the transformative power of love requires being known. In order to be known, you must learn to overcome the weight of your shame. Shame and hiddenness create distance from the love we long for and cripple us from being who we truly are. It's been that way from the beginning of humankind, and no technology, medical breakthrough, neurological discovery, or psychopharmaceutical can change this reality. We're intrinsically designed to need relationship, connection, and intimacy with other human beings.

God created Adam in his own image and recognized that it was not good for his human image-bearer to be alone. So God created another human reflecting diverse aspects of his divinity in order for the two of them to experience the deep relational knowing that occurs with God himself in the persons of the Trinity—Father, Son, Spirit. After the first man and first woman believed the serpent's lies, doubting God and believing they could be like him, they entered into an awareness of what they had just lost—the stability and safety, comfort and connection of secure attachment to God and to each other.

The very first gap (delta) emerged between what they lost—"Adam and his wife were both naked, and they felt no shame" (Genesis 2:25)—and what resulted from believing the lies—"Then the eyes of both of them were opened, and they realized they were naked" (Genesis 3:7). Keep in mind that shame emerges from the false belief that we are defective, flawed, irredeemable, unlovable. Guilt relates to what we do, but shame cuts to the heart of how we see ourselves, others, and God.

In a thousand different ways, shame whispers and shouts that being known and loved is dangerous and impossible.

If this biblical origin story doesn't resonate with you, then consider how shame took root in your life. You might remember yourself at a preschool age rushing to greet your mom or dad and tell them everything about your day. Or you might recall a time when a little kid, perhaps your own or the child of a loved one, rushed to tell you everything about themselves. As toddlers learn speech and increase their vocabulary, they discover they have a means to verbally connect with those around them. Developmentally, they move from what they learn through repetition and instruction about themselves to being known through self-disclosure.

You see this in the way a three- or four-year-old meets you and unselfconsciously begins telling you about the picture they just finger-painted, the PBJ they ate for lunch, and how their family dog licked jelly off their face. They might introduce you to dolls or action figures, describe a favorite show or movie, or want you to role-play a game of make-believe. As adults, caregivers, and parents, we wield immense power in how we respond to these invitations.

Ideally, we engage and give our undivided attention to the child before us. We ask questions and express our enjoyment through our speech, eye contact, and body language. We value the revelations being made as the child naturally seeks to be known fully and without shame. We use healthy touch to reinforce our delight in knowing the little human being sharing themselves and their world before us.

Realistically, though, most children discover that not everyone wants to know them. Sometimes it may seem as if no one wants to know them at all. If parents are busy, distracted, disengaged, addicted, or otherwise emotionally unavailable, the child's hunger to be seen, known, and valued does not go away. Continuing to reveal and share themselves soon feels futile and shameful, as if they are wanting too much from the busy adults around them. So they often stop expecting to receive the attention and sense of enjoyment they crave, either withdrawing and disappearing or disrupting and demanding attention even if critical or punitive. Depending on a number of other variables, children learn to retreat and become shy and reluctant to talk, or they tilt in the opposite direction by being louder and rambunctious.

But in light of the indifference, apathy, or criticism received from their caregivers, these children not only learned to stop trying to be known but to feel shame for wanting it.

Early in life you likely formed assumptions about the consequences of attempting to be known. Instead of being valued just for showing up and talking about whatever you wanted, you learned that mom needed you to focus on how she was feeling and to reassure her. You might have concluded that dad never engaged with you unless you achieved and excelled—in grades, sports, music, or whatever he valued. Love became conditional on your ability to parse and decipher the responses of others and become who they wanted you to be.

Your need to be known and accepted, valued and loved (Four *S*s) suddenly relied on conforming, achieving, bartering, denying, pretending, remaining silent, and lying. Being known and loved for what you do, however, makes love conditional. Love has you . . . if. Qualifying the fact that love has you then leads back to believing that it really does not have you at all. Not unconditionally. Not without strings.

## THE HOPE IN BEING KNOWN

But here's the hope in being known. Let's return for a moment to the friend with whom I shared my credit card debt. The story I told myself was that he was horrified, that I was despicable, the most irresponsible person in the world. In fact, what happened was that moments after sharing, Peter literally put his hand on my shoulder, looked me in the eyes, and said, "I cannot imagine how hard it was to share this with me." I broke into tears.

Or allow me to share a more recent example. In June 2022, after struggling with a lifetime cycle of gain-and-lose yoyo weight management attempts, I was hiking near Aspen, Colorado, with my good friend Ian. I was at my heaviest weight after Covid-19 and quarantining for months and months, eating for comfort and exercising less. We're reaching altitude over nine thousand feet, and I'm huffing and puffing and unable to keep up with Ian, who seems not to be struggling at all. My feet hurt, my ankles were swollen, and I loathed myself for being so heavy and out of shape. So I began to voice my self-contempt and shame to Ian.

His response reflected his usual caring and compassion, but it also surprised me. "I hear how much you're hating yourself right now. I know that's tough, and I want to listen. How can I support you?"

For several miles I shared about my past attempts to eat healthy and lose weight, explaining how each one failed and why I blamed myself. Ian listened carefully the whole time, and when we stopped for a water break, he said, "You've gone big in facing all your other struggles and issues, man. Why not consider going to an inpatient facility for food addiction?"

I looked at him before I burst out laughing, assuming he would as well. He didn't. Once I realized he wasn't kidding, I said, "That's the most ridiculous thing I've ever heard you say. Why would you say that?" He shrugged and we resumed our hike. "I was just throwing it out there," he said as we struggled back to the trailhead.

Later, when I told my wife, Julianne, about our conversation and Ian's suggestion, she immediately affirmed it. "I think that's the best idea I've heard for you."

One week later I was accepted into an inpatient program for eating disorders. While the timing didn't work out for me to check in right away, my acceptance allowed me to attend a twelve-step program for people with food addiction issues. There, I found a fellowship of men and women and discovered the power of the twelve steps. Within this community I discovered I wasn't alone, that I could be known in my powerlessness. I learned once again that my brokenness, powerlessness, and poverty was my admission ticket into authentic relationship, authentic connection with myself, with others, and with God. This has made all the difference.

So often we allow our fear of being known and of being rejected rather than loved to imprison us. When we don't understand why we keep doing what we're doing to be seen, soothed, safe, and secure, we're also prone to hide. We isolate ourselves and absorb even more shame.

When we are not known, when we believe the lie that love does not have us, then we die inside. Until we face that loss that feels like death, we cannot be fully reborn in the resurrection power we find in knowing Christ. Parker Palmer observed, "When we feel certain that the human soul can no longer be seen in the world, it's time to make sure that ours is visible to someone, somewhere."

Shame keeps you stuck in the delta. And not relating in vulner-ability with God and others widens the distance of the gap between the lies we believe and what is actually true. Sometimes our shame is compounded because we shame ourselves for risking vulnera-bility and hoping for acceptance rather than the perceived rejection and abandonment we believe inevitably results.

Our capacity for trust depends on our experience of the Four *S*s. We can't be known if we can't trust, and we can't trust if we haven't been seen, soothed, safe, and secure.

You experience a sense of freedom and confidence in knowing that the other person will not use the truth you disclose against you.

From this sense of trust, you feel a greater willingness to risk vulnerability, hoping that even your most shameful moments might be received without judgment, criticism, contempt, or condem-nation. Even when trust exists, vulnerability always feels like a risk because you are removing the fig leaves of success, competency, strength, power, achievement, and appearance. You're no longer relying on a protective persona or defense system to prevent entry to your shame, weakness, failure, fear, and neediness.

When you allow another person to know you as you are, your vulnerability blossoms into intimacy. As my colleague Brian Boeker likes to remind me, intimacy is when all of you welcomes all of me and all of me welcomes all of you.

I hope it's becoming clearer how the way our relationships have been formed becomes a template for our relationship with God. As you overcome the fear of being known and the accumulated shame of past pain, you connect at a deep level of acceptance, under-standing, and compassion. You enjoy the intimacy that you were designed to experience in order to heal, to grow, and to thrive. But it all begins with the practice of truth-telling.

Intimacy is built on a foundation of what's true and real.

## THE SPACE LOVE IS WAITING TO FILL

Throughout his ministry, Jesus consistently used his ability to know people as a way to dispel shame and instill grace. He refused to abide by social conventions, cultural traditions, or religious expectations. Simply put, no one could hide their heart from him, and those most aware of their shame and brokenness tended to embrace grace more quickly than those relying on merit, legalism, and appearances of good behavior.

While a myriad of changes has occurred in the two thousand years since Jesus walked on earth as a man, the human desire to be known and loved—and the shame entangling that desire—has remained the same. Christ never hesitated to minister to the outliers of Jewish society—people who today would be sex workers, drag queens, imprisoned felons, scam artists, and online trolls.

One of my favorite encounters emphasizes the power of being known—not as others know us, not even as we know ourselves, but by the power of love coming to us.

It's hard for me to mention Zacchaeus without thinking of friends who have serenaded me with the "wee little man" song from their Sunday school classes. But in fact, it's his stature that reminds us that his encounter with Jesus is all about seeing and being seen. Jesus was passing through Jericho when a certain wealthy man, a chief tax collector no less, decided he wanted to see for himself this man who claimed to be the Messiah (Luke 19:1-10). Well aware that he lacked the height to see above the crowd that had also gathered to see Jesus, Zacchaeus ran ahead and climbed a sycamore-fig tree.

From this vantage point, Zac probably thought he could observe without anyone seeing him up above them. After all, a wealthy chief tax collector might be risking a mob-mentality attack, particularly since he wasn't tall enough to defend himself very well. So perched in the tree branches, Zacchaeus probably was likely startled when

Jesus stopped, looked up, and spoke to him. He had simply planned to remain an observer, not the observed.

"Zacchaeus, come down immediately. I must stay at your house today," Jesus yelled up. And without hesitation, this wee little man "came down at once and welcomed him gladly" (Luke 19:5-6). Once the onlookers realized whom Jesus had chosen to dine with, their shame detectors got set off. "He has gone to be the guest of a sinner," they said (Luke 19:7). Notice the double slam here—not only is Zacchaeus an outright sinner, but Jesus has chosen to be his guest, telling everyone all they needed to know about both of them.

But shame had no power to prevent Zacchaeus from realizing the truth that he was seen, known, and loved as he was, not for his reputation based on behavior.

The little man wasted no time proclaiming the extent of his restitution in making up for his ill-earned wealth. In reply, Jesus commented on the truth of Zac's identity and the truth of his own: "Today salvation has come to this house, because this man, too, is a son of Abraham. For the Son of Man came to seek and to save the lost" (Luke 19:9-10). Zac was wretched—lost, wandering, without a home, without resources. And Jesus came to restore what was lost.

Basically, none of those observing could claim to be any better than this man they saw as a corrupt government con artist intent on stealing from them to benefit himself. Zacchaeus was just as much a descendant of Israel's patriarch as the rest of them. Referring to himself as the Son of Man, Jesus repeated a frequent refrain of his purpose—he was there to seek and to save what was lost, those willing to be seen and known even in their shame.

We have the same opportunity to be seen and known by God and by others if we're willing to risk and opt for vulnerability and to align our lives with love.

The process requires acknowledging our limitations, admitting our mistakes, facing the consequences of those we've wounded, and abiding in a power greater than our own.

The power of love that meets us where we are.

Whether that's up in a tree.

In a seedy adult bookstore.

At the kitchen counter with a gallon of ice cream at 2 a.m.

Shifting money from your credit card to a sports betting app to cover your losses.

Online with scenes that arouse without ever satisfying.

No matter where you are, refuse to let shame occupy the space love is waiting to fill.

**BLESSING**

*May you courageously risk being known as you are.*
*May you experience the power of love*
*as you risk vulnerability.*
*May you know that God sees you, knows you, accepts you,*
*and loves you—right where you are.*

# 9

# MYSTICISM

## EXPERIENCING SPIRITUAL ONENESS WITH GOD

*The devout Christian of the future will either be a "mystic," one who has experienced "something," or he will cease to be anything at all.*

KARL RAHNER

In my experience, returning to familiar places from childhood reveals how I've changed more than how the place has changed. Such was the case when returning to Carmel of the Holy Family in Cleveland Heights, Ohio, to visit my aunt, Sister Anne, a Carmelite nun. You'll recall how my childhood visits, one in particular, made indelible memories of being transported from one world to another, from the outside parlor with my parents and siblings to the inner sanctum, where my aunt and other nuns delighted in my arrival as if I'd been dropped off by a divine stork.

As I matured into adolescence and then college, I no longer had to tag along when my parents visited her. I wrote to my aunt occasionally, and she kindly remembered me with a card, note, bookmark, or picture on my birthday, at Christmas and Easter, and on my namesake saint's day, Michaelmas, Saint Michael's Day, September 29. While my inherited Catholic faith faded, my newfound more Protestant faith solidified and grew. So much so that in my

late twenties I felt compelled to visit my aunt and the other nuns
whom I remembered so fondly from my harrowing childhood.

Pulling up to the convent housing the Carmelites in an older
suburban neighborhood, I found it shrunken a few sizes, its ginger-
bread trimmings sagging. My aunt, along with Sister Jean Marie
and Sister Bernadette, welcomed me warmly, eager to see the man
I had become.

Their gentleness and hospitality had not changed, and they
quizzed me on my life, eager to hear about my beautiful new wife,
my studies in Colorado, and my awareness of God's calling to be a
counselor. I answered them honestly but also in a way that revealed
the subtle superiority of my more theologically based, biblically
accurate view of God and faith. I defaulted to impressing them with
my knowledge of church history, explaining why Catholicism had
failed to sustain my view of God and the world. I needed more
Bible and couldn't accept the authority of tradition.

If they detected my condescension, they didn't show it, and as
I drove away a couple hours later, I felt proud of how my faith had
evolved. That I was no longer contained by the liturgy and doctrine, by centuries of corruption and political policies, by a hier-
archy that now seemed unbiblical and indefensible. While I didn't
acknowledge it as such, a part of me pitied my aunt and her Carmelite sisters, wasting away in their cloistered lives of prayer and
devoted supplication.

Thinking of my arrogance and self-righteousness some thirty
years later, I cringe.

Shame gut-punches me with the audacity of my condescending
pity and, ironically, what I now see clearly as their rock-solid, un-
wavering faith and a love for me that refused to condemn me for my
self-absorbed entitlement. Looking back, I realize that I didn't understand the mystery of faith. And so I dismissed their mysticism, their

commitment to experiencing intimacy with God without having to have all the answers.

Now, I cannot imagine my faith without it.

### MYSTERY OF FAITH

Entering adulthood, I lost myself in my addictions. The horrific impact of my childhood abuse, emotional neglect, and deprivation kept me stuck in a sense of chaos that was beyond overwhelming. Consequently, I wanted a faith that could restore emotional and relational order, make sense of what made no sense, and provide spiritual stability and security. I wanted to manage my relationship with God, making sure I would never fall from his good graces.

This was the closest thing I knew to what I now recognize as secure attachment with God, and I assumed an intellectual and academic approach could create that.

Instead, it had the opposite effect. Out of my desire to know God, I traded my experience of him for an intellectual understanding of him, or at least an attempt to contain him theologically rather than the unpredictability of a relationship.

It's the difference between an orphan reading a book on parenting versus being welcomed by a loving individual fully engaged in knowing, accepting, affirming, and loving that orphan.

I worked hard, so incredibly hard, to know God and please him and achieve the kind of relationship I wanted—basically, the kind that made sense and conformed to working in a way that consistently provided what I thought I wanted and needed. But like trying to force myself to be in love with someone I didn't actually know and only knew about, I failed in my objective. Thank God, I failed in my objective! He loves me too much to let me sink into the smug quicksand of systematic containment of what can never be contained.

It took beating my aching head against the walls of the church for many years before I glimpsed the simple truth behind the temple curtain. Sanctification is called the *mystery* of faith for a reason. Salvation relies on a personal relationship with God in order to define the essence of that mystery. Embracing this divine relationship by experiencing him nourishes and sustains one's faith. Someone who pursues this inner experience of knowing and relating with God is a Christian mystic.

Mysticism, by this definition, is therefore a necessity for faith. Mysticism is not about the extremes you might be tempted to tilt toward, not the esoteric, totally subjective wanderings of the mind into a spiritual realm, and not the holy union of human and divine reserved only for nuns and monks, devoted supplicants and sacred visionaries. Mysticism is spiritual breathing for the soul. It's as essential for the health of our spirits as oxygen is for our bodies.

When considering how, as a mystic, to experience God, we usually arrive at the three ways described by Meister Eckhart, the renowned fourteenth-century theologian, philosopher, and mystic. The first method of knowing God is through our five senses. Through direct sensations of our physical bodies, we glimpse God's creative imagination, unlimited power, and pleasurable presence—in the blood-orange sunset soaking the horizon with streaks of gold and magenta, as a baby coos to her mother's lullaby, on the lavender breeze wafting through an open window, by the enveloping embrace of a best friend, the first sip of coffee each morning.

The second means of experiencing God is through intellectual pursuit. Unfortunately, as I found out firsthand, this method often supersedes any others. This approach has also become the default setting for us in the twenty-first century. Our intellects collect and analyze, sort and process so much and cannot be dismissed. It simply cannot be expected to be our only way of experiencing and knowing.

Using science and medicine, logic and reason, theology and cosmology, we learn about the brilliant intricacy of God's care in crafting the human body and the neural pathways of the brain, the myriad oceanic life forms and the sparkling grandeur of the cosmos. More and more frequently, doctors and scientists continue realizing the overlapping truths of science and spirituality. God is literally in the details.

Finally, Eckhart posited humans can experience God through their ability to unite their spirit with the great divine Spirit. Beyond the physical and intellectual methods, spiritual knowing emerges from deep inside our being, beyond our ego, our rationale, our emotions. This may be perhaps the essence of a mystical experience with our Creator, learning to get out of our own way in attempting to quantify and qualify, contain and conscript God to our usual ways of knowing.

Knowing God through spiritual intimacy includes our heart, our soul, our spirit. Guided by God's Spirit within us, we activate what Eckhart described as the "divine spark" or "eternal now" within each human being, the transcendently divine essence of God in each person, the love that longs to unite with Love, to give love away to those in need of knowing Love.

Letting go of our attachments such as achievement, wealth, power, and fame, we discover our authentic selves. This kind of detachment from these outcomes allows us to surrender to love, to attach to the union that is already there, to experience the loving presence that already surrounds us.

All three methods—our senses, our intellect, and our spirit—serve as conduits for knowing God in a deeply personal and intimate way. Through them we fulfill the command Jesus gave us: "Love the Lord your God with all your heart and with all your soul and with all your mind" (Matthew 22:37). In other words, mysticism is nothing if not practical.

## HOLY HIDE-AND-SEEK

If you thought mysticism was just an abstract, perhaps archaic, practice limited to supernatural saints with remarkable life circumstances recorded in the annals of church history, then it's time to think again. I'm convinced exploring and embracing the practices of mysticism is the key to closing the gap between belief and experience.

For many if not most people, the greatest barrier to experiencing God in this deeply personal and transformative way is his hiddenness. While we can know him through our senses, it's often through his creation. While we can know him by encountering him intellectually, mysticism and intellectualism are not the same as relating intimately. Which leaves us to explore and discover knowing him at a much more sublime and sacred level, which often frustrates us because it seems so indefinable, so subjective, so squishy and elusive.

We wonder why it seems so challenging and often frustrating to experience God the way we long to know him. We wonder if he intentionally wants to remain hidden from us and if so, for what reasons. Does he want to draw us closer by remaining somewhat elusive? What's his motive for all the holy hide-and-seek?

The theologically correct answer for many is that God's hiddenness requires us to live by faith. If God appeared physically and related to us as we desire, then faith would be unnecessary. So what is it about faith that God apparently views as essential to knowing him?

As my own faith beliefs and practices began to come apart at the seams of experience, I began searching for different answers to the age-old questions about the importance of faith in knowing

God. While I did not find a definitive answer, instead I discovered a treasure chest of insight and wisdom from practitioners of the faith known historically as mystics, including John of the Cross, Bernard of Clairvaux, Theresa of Ávila, Julian of Norwich, and Thérèse of Lisieux.

They don't claim to have the answer but draw on their own inner experiences to describe and reflect how they know God and believe he wants to be known. Much of what they describe reflects the tension between our mortality in human bodies and God's immortality as the three-in-one Godhead. Basically, our human attempts to know God pivot on the paradox that the more deeply we know anything, the more the subject of our knowing becomes less conceptually clear. We lose the forest by focusing on the tree before us. Objects may appear closer than they actually are.

But this doesn't preclude us from getting our bearings.

From gaining some idea of where we are.

And taking first steps on a new journey of discovery.

### KNOWING THE UNKNOWABLE

If you're willing to explore knowing God in a new, uncharted direction, then you can learn much by following the trail markers of those who have entered this spiritual wilderness before you. While they may not provide the precision and clarity you desire, they can offer some benchmarks and signposts indicating you're aiming in the right direction. These trailblazers illuminate and innovate, inviting us into our own unique encounters with the divine.

One of the classic and best-known written works of spiritual mysticism is *The Cloud of Unknowing*. Likely written in Middle English during the fourteenth century, this collection of writings by an unknown author(s) invites readers to know God by letting go of what they think they know and instead entering into the realm of what they do not, and perhaps cannot, know through human senses and intellect.

Before assuming this lofty, abstract way relies on consuming mushrooms or other psychedelics, you might find three analogies drawn from this classic work helpful in providing access to the paradox of knowing the unknowable. The following descriptions are based on Ronald Rolheiser's reflective explanations in "The Hiddenness of God and the Darkness of Faith."

The first metaphor is that of a baby within the mother's womb. During pregnancy, the infant cannot see or experience the mother except from within. The mother is of course present—so much so in her nurturing provision to her child that the baby cannot know her separately and independently until after the birthing process.

Similarly, what if we, like this unborn infant, can only know God from within our relational union with him? We're told in the Scriptures that in God we live and move and have our being (Acts 17:28). We know God as we grow and develop and mature as he intends but remain limited by our human condition during our time in this life. We are born again, a spiritual birth when we experience and embrace his divine love through Jesus, in preparation for the life to come beyond our earthly existence.

The second analogy draws on the relationship between darkness and light. For instance, you may have witnessed one of the historic eclipses that have taken place in recent years. Watching the sun required protection for your eyes because otherwise the intense concentration of its light would blind you. Staring directly into the brightest light from the sun would result in blindness and its inherent darkness.

Perhaps, just as staring into sunlight would only blind us, knowing God fully as he is would render us incapable of knowing him. Consider Moses in the Old Testament experiencing God as a burning bush. Or the followers of Jesus at Pentecost who received

God's presence through the gift of the Holy Spirit descending on them as a tongue of flame. Fire would normally consume and destroy us with the intensity of its heat incinerating us, yet spiritually it symbolizes God's presence. What if what we often experience as darkness is merely our inability to withstand the brilliant intensity of God's being?

Finally, the third comparison to consider is more relational. Think about the people closest to you, the ones you know best who also know you. Try to recall the first time you met your spouse or one of your best friends. What was your first impression? How did you view them and assess them based on their appearance and the other information available? On context? As you became more intimately acquainted with them, your objectivity dissolved. You began to know them intimately, which necessitated losing perspective based merely on appearances and facts.

Knowing God often works the same way. Perhaps you struggled in your faith even for this very reason. You knew a lot about God but still did not actually know God. You might have studied the Bible, learned ancient languages, read and learned from great rabbis and theologians. But none of those endeavors necessarily resulted in relating directly and intimately with God. Knowing and relating requires your willingness to be fully vulnerable before him and in return seek to know him in the fullness of who he is as expressed by the Trinity.

## INTO THE MYSTIC

As you begin to reconsider and redefine mysticism for yourself, some gleanings from other seekers, pilgrims, and followers of Christ can help you. These are not keys or secrets, not progressive steps or a spiritual formula for mystical success. They are simply nine rather ordinary truths that I like to think of as Mystical Considerations:

1. *Mysticism is inherently subjective, poetic, intuitive, imaginative, and experiential.* It's difficult to fit into any theological or psychological box, and a wide variety of spiritual seekers have claimed to experience God and find truth through events or practices that they deemed mystical.

2. *You won't find the word* mysticism *in the Bible; however, you will find the word* mystery. Paul calls believers to be "stewards of God's mysteries" (1 Corinthians 4:1 NRSV). In fact, throughout the New Testament, references to the "mystery of God" and the "mystery of Christ" emerge. While there's no way to fully solve or resolve these mysteries, they point back to who God is, who he made us to be, and how we know him.

3. *Mysticism holds the tension between knowing God and experiencing him through his absence.* One reason the "cloud of unknowing" illustrates this paradox so well is because it takes something familiar and known—a cloud—and describes its essence as being unknowable. Just as you cannot engineer your way to a relationship with God, you cannot come up with an algorithm for expressing mysticism. Or consider this: when a close friend or family member moves away, you still know them and realize aspects of who they are and what you love about them . . . which then get reshaped by the next time you see them in person.

4. *Language is inadequate to express mysticism*, which is ineffable and cannot be accurately rendered in words. This does not exclude discussing mysticism with others nor the ability to communicate with God. After all, Paul describes how the Holy Spirit often prays within us and for us with "sighs too deep for words" (Romans 8:26 NRSV). Perhaps this also reflects why poetry, always an experiential whole greater than

the sum of its parts, comes closer than prose to conveying one's experience of God.

5. *Symbolism, simile, metaphor, allegory, parable, and analogy help us to reflect, express, and convey mysticism.* Consider the way the cross has been appropriated to represent the death and resurrection of Jesus, worn by countless people and adorning the walls and altars of various churches and places of worship. We also have Jesus using bread and wine to create the sacrament of Communion that continues to represent how he nourishes and sustains us. Water used in baptism also depicts the inner cleansing we experience by grace through the love of God in Christ.

6. *Mysticism often makes the church and institutional religion very uncomfortable* because it cannot be regulated, controlled, explained precisely, and aligned uniformly. Throughout the centuries, particularly in the Catholic and liturgical traditions, men and women have practiced mysticism as a means of experiencing God and knowing him. But the inherent subjectivity and impossibility of regulating mysticism caused problems, mostly between individuals and institutions. While some mystics were leaders and well regarded, others were considered heretical and criminal. Without the ability to codify mysticism into a specific doctrine or dogmatic diagram, those in power may feel threatened by the intrinsic spiritual power afforded to individuals rather than congregations and religious hierarchies. As societies and cultures shift, views of those who experience God through mysticism often change over time. Yesterday's heretics are today's saints! Thomas Aquinas was condemned in his lifetime by the bishop of Paris but is now highly regarded as a thought leader of the church and practitioner of contemplative faith. Others

such as Pierre Teilhard de Chardin, Thomas Merton, and Meister Eckhart are now accepted by many as exemplars of mysticism, while others remain skeptical and critical.

7. *Rather than supernatural visions, miraculous events, and extraordinary encounters, mysticism relies more on being present to the mundane, the small, the everyday, and the ordinary.* While saints such as Francis of Assisi and Julian of Norwich are known for phenomenal, almost fairy-tale-like events in their lives, they pointed to a humble attitude, basic provisions, and consistent practices as indicative of a mystical lifestyle. Certainly, mystics throughout the centuries warn us not to make miracles and visions our goal but rather byproducts of our deeply personal connection with God.

8. *Mysticism, while often practiced in solitude and silence, is always relational,* seeking to serve and minister to others. Even the ancient fathers and mothers who became hermits by retreating to the desert or mountains continued to teach and instruct those they encountered as well as pray for countless others. In fact, their rule of life required them to welcome strangers and show hospitality and engage in relationship with their guests and visitors. They only withdrew from the world in order to enter into a deeper experience of God. But mystics never overlooked their human need for connection and community, often dwelling in monasteries, convents, artists' colonies, religious orders, and communal living facilities.

9. *Mysticism is characterized by holy optimism and overflow—* joy, peace, delight, reverie, worship, praise, fellowship, felicity, and hospitality. Mysticism seeks to cultivate, harvest, and share the fruits of the Spirit. Rather than being bound by duty, obligation, commands, and laws, mysticism relies on

the freedom found in God's grace as experienced through the power of his divine love. When love has you, you manifest and share all the gifts he has placed within you.

## NEW OLD WAYS

When I look back on my visit to my aunt and the sisters of Carmel, my sadness and disappointment in myself are eclipsed by even greater admiration for their example of a loving, vibrant faith. The very qualities I then considered unbiblical, outdated, and irrelevant are the ones I now know are holy, timeless, and urgently relevant. Their ability to love me despite my air of legalism and self-righteousness has had a greater impact on my faith than any sermon or Sunday school lesson.

At some point in my journey, as systems and theology and knowledge about God were no longer enough, I began to accept, "If that's what a mystic is, then I'm a mystic!" I could relinquish the rubble of past constraints, false beliefs, and limiting assumptions and move forward in reconstructing the foundational faith that remained within me. I could step out of the shadow of past spiritual abuse and begin to experience healing in the presence of love.

This deeply personal shift was not without challenges and conflicts. Even as I opened my mind and heart to new (yet ancient) ways of experiencing God, even as I redefined my understanding of mysticism, I still wanted more concrete practices and clear-cut instructions. I wanted to know what it looks like, how I should go about it, and what particular practices to pursue. Which led me to explore our greatest human asset in experiencing God—our imagination (the focus of our next chapter)—before adopting various spiritual practices and making them my own.

If my process resonates, then I hope you are open to reconsidering your definition of mysticism. And if the uncomfortable, disruptive, loosey-goosey, woo-woo notion of mysticism still lingers, that's okay. Because your mysticism will not be like anyone else's. It will be the native language of your soul in conversation with the divine heart of God.

It takes time to relax into anything new and different and unfamiliar. But over time, as you encounter others on the same pursuit, you will realize that you all share the same alphabet of grace, the silent poetry of joy embodied when love has you. You will experience intimacy with God.

## BLESSING

*May you close the gap between belief and experience*
*as you explore the mystery of faith.*
*May you surrender ways of seeing God and practices*
*that limit your relationship with him.*
*May you experience God's love in ways uniquely personal*
*and divinely attuned.*

# 10

# IMAGINATION

## LEARNING TO SEE WITH THE EYES
## OF THE HEART

*Nearly all that I loved I believed to be imaginary; nearly all that
I believed to be real I thought grim and meaningless.*

C. S. LEWIS

"Willy Wonka took my last dollar—that's when I hit rock bottom."

I looked at my client—a smiling, successful novelist and screenwriter who came to me about his gambling addiction—and held his gaze with my best poker face. Which seemed appropriate as he shared the way visiting casinos and playing backroom Texas hold'em had cost him everything—his savings, his advance against his next bestseller, his home, and ultimately his wife and young children. With each loss and setback, he somehow found more capital to pour into his futile efforts. We had discussed the way the unknowably random thrill of winning was an addiction unlike any other, each hit teasing the big payoff of a dopamine jackpot.

After going through his high-roller phase, this man began lowering his wagers and even doing something he swore he would never do—playing slot machines. While my mental image of a slot machine resembles an old-fashioned cash register spewing quarters, the new models he described were more like high-tech video games. No longer rolling cherries, stars, and bars, new slots relied on technology for immersive sights and sounds, systems and schematics. Today's slot machines were virtual experiences, often exploiting nostalgia, celebrities, iconic music, and beloved movies and TV characters—everything from Dolly Parton to *Game of Thrones.*

"From across the casino, I heard Gene Wilder singing 'Pure Imagination' and started feeling so emotional," he said. "I got up and started following the sound until it led me to this enormous station with four padded chairs, each with its own giant flat screen where sound bites from my favorite childhood movie, *Willie Wonka & the Chocolate Factory*, enticed me with all the sadness and joy of being a kid again."

He sat there pushing buttons for three hours, feeding hundred-dollar bills from his only remaining credit card's final cash advance. By 2 a.m., he had lost two thousand dollars and left humming the Oompa Loompa song. Two months later, after accepting a gig ghostwriting, he was ready to face the truth of his struggle and came to see me.

"You know what I hate the most?" he said wistfully. "Pimping my imagination."

## PURE IMAGINATION

My client's story lingered with me as I recalled my childhood joy at watching Gene Wilder's Willie Wonka lead his Golden Ticket winners on a journey to face their hearts' desires for immediate gratification. The blend of silly and surreal, of the goodness of Charlie Bucket and the spoiled selfishness of the other kids, left me reeling. The happy ending in the Great Glass Elevator as Charlie is entrusted as Wonka's successor.

But what made the biggest impression on me was indeed the power of the imagination. The way children use their imaginations with unbridled, unselfconscious joy. The way Willie Wonka relied on it as the nuclear engine of his candy-coated empire. Rather than pursue greater sales and consumer brand identity, Wonka focused on innovation. On creating what he envisioned in his imagination. On learning from attempts that didn't quite work. On Technicoloring outside the lines of convention.

When I consider the power of the imagination, I think about Michelangelo carving away marble until only his vision remained or about Walt Disney imagining Disneyland into existence and later Disney World, which was not completed until after his death. I recall the observation made by Antoine de Saint-Exupéry: "A rock pile ceases to be a rock pile the moment a single man contemplates it, bearing within him the image of a cathedral."

For mystics, spiritual pilgrims, and followers of Jesus of Nazareth, the power of the imagination was once paramount to their experience of God. Because the Christian faith relies on and revolves around the invisible, the Spirit-infused imagination ushered them deeper into God's transcendent kingdom. They understood Paul's prayer to believers at Ephesus: "I pray that the eyes of your heart may be enlightened in order that you may know the hope to which he has called you, the riches of his glorious inheritance in his holy people" (Ephesians 1:18).

Intrinsic to our relationship with God, we are created and invited to see with the eyes of the heart. We pray and sing Paul Baloche's lyrics, "Open the eyes of my heart, Lord. I want to see you." Metaphorically, I cannot think of a better way to describe the imagination than the vision emanating from the deep center of our being.

But what if this way of seeing is not simply fixing our focus on God, but a way of seeing all of reality, all of God's transcendent truth? With the eyes of our heart, we see who we really are and who God really is, dispelling the first two deceptions back in Eden.

Such clarity allows us to see others with the gaze of our heart through the lens of love as well.

If the imagination is so important, then why has it been side-lined and sublimated to the intellect and willpower? Why do we not cultivate our imagination in order to see more fully and clearly? Like other unwieldy aspects of faith, the imagination became dangerous to church leaders and political powerbrokers. The imagination asked too many questions, considered too many possibilities, refused to conform to religious rules, and saw what they could not. The imagination was too subjective and creative, too ethereal and unlimited. And yet it's with the imagination that we see reality.

Instead, the church emphasized the power of the will and the importance of the intellect. Particularly after the Renaissance and into the Industrial Revolution, shaping the mind to manage behavior became a spiritual priority. Emphasizing doctrine and dogma and intellectual understanding became the religious priority. The imagination was left to children and lunatics, to artists and poets, to outliers and outcasts. After all, fantasy—a vital part of the imagination's engine—could lead one into temptation and beyond if allowed to thrive. Fiction and fairy tales were sidelined and replaced by sober stories of saints and prayer books filled with creeds and commands.

Dismissing the imagination's vital role in cultivating personal faith, however, results in a faith that's lacking and limited. Consider the result if fire had been banished or electricity unplugged because of the potential damage they might unleash. As you begin to live in the fullness of love and experience God in deeper, more vivid and relevant ways, you cannot ignore the imagination.

Mysticism relies on the imagination, not as a danger or threat, but as a portal to the divine. When you have surrendered yourself to God, your imagination is sanctified along with the rest of you.

God designed us with this unique ability to create because he wanted us to be made in his image. To experience the thrill of seeing what no one else can see and then bring new life and light to what was once dark and shapeless. Before you begin considering spiritual practices that close the gap between your beliefs and reality, you would do well to befriend your imagination.

## THE SACRED IMAGINATION

Much of the modern Western Christian mindset relies on gathering information and data in order to know God more fully and understand his ways. Therefore, knowing God means studying the Bible, learning about ancient histories and cultures, languages and customs. Growing in faith then requires becoming a better student who acquires more biblical knowledge, memorizes Scripture, understands theology, and studies church history.

As you have most likely experienced, this approach only goes so far toward knowing God and experiencing relationship with him. It's appealing to believe we know what we have to do in order to be a "better Christian" and follower of Jesus, but that approach also sets us up for disappointment, derailment, and deconstruction. Because knowledge is never an adequate substitute for experience. Insight and information cannot change a human heart. Relying on your intellect, on ways of comprehending or analyzing information that's rational and logical, fails because it segregates your humanity and your spirituality.

C. S. Lewis, with his brilliant mind and academic education, assumed there could be no God in a world filled with the kind of suffering evident in a world shattered by two world wars. Reflecting on his time as an atheist, he wrote, "The two hemispheres of my mind were in the sharpest contrast. On the one side a many-islanded sea of poetry and myths: on the other a glib and shallow 'rationalism.' Nearly all that I loved I believed to be imaginary; nearly all that I believed to be real I thought grim and meaningless."

Lewis, of course, later experienced God and embraced the mystery of faith in ways that liberated his fantastical imagination, resulting in the Chronicles of Narnia series of novels and the Space Trilogy, along with other powerful works of fiction and many insightful nonfiction books. He realized the power of the imagination to convey truth in ways that bypassed and transcended the rational mind without alienating it altogether. Narnia depicts a world brimming with surreal elements, magical powers, and mythological creatures, but the messages and themes always lead back to grace, to the power of forgiveness and mercy, to the extraordinary hope found in God's divine love for his children.

Lewis harnessed the power of the imagination and the appeal of archetypal story in order to reflect the gospel message in unique and startling ways, captivating adults and children alike. His fictional work provides a way to embody and experience the instruction Jesus gave to his followers, "Truly I tell you, unless you change and become like little children, you will never enter the kingdom of heaven" (Matthew 18:3).

Children see the world around them open to possibilities, not limited by their physical senses. When we were kids, we delighted in the power of story to enthrall our minds and hearts with tales of princes and princesses, dragons and unicorns, talking animals and singing objects. The conduit for our delight resided in the portal of our imagination.

As we mature into adulthood, however, we're often conditioned to focus on and trust in only what we can see, define, measure, quantify, and categorize tangibly and concretely.

In order to reconstruct our faith, to close the gap between our beliefs and our experience, the imagination must be reclaimed and relied on as the ignition of our mystical experience of God.

## BEAUTY AND SUFFERING

Iain McGilchrist, a psychiatrist, Oxford-trained literary scholar, and philosopher, describes the shift required for us to reactivate the role of our imagination. According to him, we need "a way of looking at the world quite different from the one that has largely dominated the west for at least 350 years. . . . We've depended on that aspect of our brains that is most adept at manipulating the world in order to bend it to our purpose. Then we take our success in manipulating it as proof we understand it."

He explains how the left hemisphere of the human brain focuses on certainty, while the right hemisphere is about possibility. The left seeks to apprehend (and thus manipulate the world), while the right hemisphere tries to comprehend (seeing the world for all it is). It is the right brain that mediates insight and receptivity, intuition and spirituality—and not surprisingly, attachment.

While these dual functions are designed to work in tandem, most individuals tend to rely on one more than the other, resulting in the generalized view of right-brain creatives and left-brain analysts.

Make no mistake: One is not superior or inferior to the other. Both hemispheres are necessary. When it comes to matters of faith, however, the right brain cannot be detached, sublimated, or ignored. Faith, inherent to its definition, believes and acts on what is beyond our human senses and limitations: "Now faith is confidence in what we hope for and assurance about what we do not see" (Hebrews 11:1).

Considering this basic understanding of faith, how can we live with God without imagination? You'll recall that early on, I referred to our nature to grasp at love rather than passively receive it. The way we open ourselves to God's presence, power, love, peace, grace, and the limitless person of who he is relies on our imagination. Not because God isn't real, but because he is *so real* that we need the eyes of our heart in order to see, know, experience him. His divine reality transcends and supersedes the reality to which we're limited here on earth.

We must elevate and integrate imagination as a crucial component of our faith and any life with God. Sounds simple enough, right? After all, we engage our imagination every day as we watch memes, TV shows, and movies, as we listen to music, discussions, and sound bites—even gaming. Our imagination transports us into other worlds, other people, other lives and circumstances, other time periods and cultures.

Taken up a notch, our imaginations are stimulated, provoked, nourished, and challenged by those sensual experiences in which our awareness of the present moment becomes heightened. Simply put, beauty becomes self-evident, arresting our imagination with something that cannot be ignored. Something evoking emotion and bypassing thought at first, something appealing to our senses, to our awareness of the present.

We cannot help but respond to the extraordinary beauty of the Grand Canyon, a beach at sunset, the Sistine Chapel, or Monet's haystacks shifting in seasonal light. We revel in music by Mozart, the latest song from our favorite artist, or the blended voices of a choir. But we are delighted daily, hourly, to partake of ordinary beauty as well. To pause and smile on hearing the coo of a baby, to notice the variegated shift from green to scarlet in an autumn leaf, the scent of freshly ground coffee brewing, the loving caress of our spouse.

Beauty is not the only dream catcher of the imagination. Suffering often stops us in our tracks and demands our attention in similar fashion. Simone Weil noted that only beauty and affliction can pierce the human heart.

Suffering, that sense of spinning free of the gravity of our default lives, seems self-evident as well. And not just extraordinary suffering such as battling cancer, grieving the death of a loved one, overcoming anxiety and fear during a pandemic, but the ordinary suffering we encounter just as frequently as moments of daily beauty. We are invited to enter into the ordinary suffering of unmet longings and smaller disappointments, of frustration over speeding tickets and toilets that overflow, the sting of a coworker's harsh comment or the critical comment on social media.

Ordinary suffering often accretes and accumulates, becoming the suffering of anxiety and depression, the low-grade fever of painful disappointment gradually rising to the more urgent disease requiring distraction, escape, pleasure, comfort, and relief.

We seek out places and opportunities, relationships and recreation to provide what we lack in longing to be seen, soothed, safe, and secure.

Harnessed to our suffering alone, the imagination operates to provide counterfeits and fantasies, inferior versions of what we were created to experience and enjoy.

When we lose sight of our need and capacity for beauty, we starve our imagination, leaving it to binge and purge on the highs of addiction, the illicit power of porn-fueled orgasms, the fantasies spun by pretending to be both more and less than we are.

The imagination is fueled most powerfully by beauty and suffering, which rivet our attention like few other things, but paradoxically, the reality of God is demonstrated most powerfully by beauty and suffering joined together in the crucifixion. Where the cross of Christ holds both brutality and sacrifice, injustice and grace, the fulfillment of the Law through the power of love surrendered. The cross was both an instrument of execution and also the bridge to divine love.

Your imagination allows you to grasp both of these truths at once. That's part of its power.

But where your imagination takes you depends on where you want to go.

## SOMETHING HOLY SHINING THROUGH

Your imagination is a crucial pathway to knowing God. No one would take issue with the fact that faith requires imagining something invisible. Hope requires imagining something that does not yet exist. And love requires imagining that we engage in imaginative acts of service to others and the world.

Activation of your spiritual imagination requires vertical alignment to maximize its full divine potential. Vertical alignment to engage with what is most real. Upward attunement with God's love.

When only aimed horizontally at beauty and pleasure or at suffering and escape, our imagination runs at half capacity. God gave us the gift of imagination in order to know and experience him and his goodness. In order to activate this capacity and maximize its divine potential, we must unite it with his love. This upward attunement occurs when we nourish and sustain our imagination with truth and beauty, the story of God, and other good stories, relationships with others, and connections to the natural world.

Our sanctified imagination allows us to understand reality, ultimate truth, beyond what we can know with our human senses and mortal limitations. It allows us to experience revelation and epiphany, an unconcealing of God's truth and beauty, rather than become preoccupied with correct answers and acceptable theology. Through regular exercise and practice, our imagination magnifies our ability to see what is real and to deepen our attachment to loving presence. We learn to rely on the eyes of our heart as much if not more than the eyes of our body.

Malcolm Guite, an Anglican poet, priest, and fellow at Cambridge, describes how our imagination can lift the veil of what is visible to human eyes, revealing the invisible kingdom of God's lavish love. He notes, "Samuel Taylor Coleridge, the great poet and

theologian of the imagination, says that he and William Wordsworth were using the arts to awaken the mind's attention, to help
us, just as much as science might help us, to look out and see what
is really there and to discover that reality is itself numinous, trans-
lucent with glimmerings of the 'supernatural,' of something holy
shining through it."

And it is with the imagination that we see the holy shining through.

Guite, like the "theologians of the imagination" who have inspired him, urges us to pay attention to the present by looking at
the world through the lens of our imagination. Not to escape or
fantasize, not to reshape or revise, but simply to see what is there.
To see God more clearly and to take in the panorama of holiness
unfolding around us every moment of every day. To stop trying to
do so much and learn so much and to still ourselves and receive
divine love through our divine receptor, our imagination.

When we allow our imagination to guide us closer to God, we
can experience him in ways that are deeply personal, intimate, and
transformative. I recall going to hear Brennan Manning speak at a
small Episcopal church in Denver almost thirty years ago. He
spoke about God in such familiar and familial ways that I couldn't
help but envy his closeness with God. Given the chance to speak
with Brennan following his talk, I shared my desire for the kind of
intimacy with God evident in his life.

Not surprisingly, he explained how the way he knew God was
far from exclusive—it was the way God longs to be known by each
and every one of his children, as a loving papa running to welcome
us back no matter how far away we may feel or might have strayed.
Later, I had another opportunity to hear Brennan speak at a spiritual retreat, and he asked us to pray with him. He led us on a kind
of guided meditation to a still, quiet place within, a place of longing
and expectancy.

There, lulled by his lilting voice, I was invited to imagine Jesus sitting there with us. To notice how Jesus beckoned me to come closer to him and then closer still, sitting beside and leaning into him. Then he gently put his arm around me. As my tears began to spill down my cheeks, I was invited to lay my head in Jesus' lap, the way a small boy might find comfort from his dad or mom.

That experience transformed the way I thought about prayer and Jesus and my relationship to God. I realized that through the power of my imagination, I could enjoy a kind of closeness that felt every bit as real as a friend's hand on my shoulder. Although it would take me many more years to free my imagination more consistently in experiencing God, I was no longer satisfied with relying on knowledge and theology, on studying ancient languages and hermeneutics. I wanted to be held. And I wanted to behold. I wanted to rest my head in Jesus' lap without any reason other than it's what everything in my being longed to do.

Perhaps you've had a similar experience in life, while praying or meditating or simply stilling yourself in order to pay attention and notice God. That same kind of connection is available to you right now and for the rest of your life through the power of the imagination. It's not your fantasy of being held by God but the truest reality. Your capacity to experience in this moment may be affected by the extent to which you've been seen, soothed, safe, and secure. This kind of connection, however, is your spiritual birthright, which is not a fantasy but reality. It's the way you express and cultivate and convey that love has you. And will never let you go.

Only by our imagination can we know that love has us.

## BLESSING

*May you see the invisible reality of love with*
*the eyes of your heart.*
*May you develop the joy of childlike faith through*
*the power of your imagination.*
*May all that is holy continue to shine through*
*your imagination as it aligns with love.*

*11*

# PRACTICE

EMBODYING OUR CONNECTION WITH GOD

*Grace is opposed to earning, not to effort.*

DALLAS WILLARD

I never thought I would get a tattoo, let alone two.

When my young adult son moved out of our home, however, he reminded me that I had promised him I'd get a tattoo before he left. I admired his tats and liked the idea of having one myself, but I had never felt passionate enough about anything that I would want it marked permanently on my body. Faced with honoring the commitment to my son, I wanted a word or symbol that would provide an ongoing reminder of something significant.

By the time my son and I arrived at the tattoo shop, I knew what I wanted. The hardest command in the Bible for me to obey comes from Psalm 46:10—to be still and to know the love of God. So I decided to remind myself to do the two spiritual practices that I found most personally challenging. On my right arm I had *BE STILL* indelibly written, while my left arm reminds me to *BE LOVED*. I chose their placement to be equally as meaningful. Because I'm right-handed, I wanted to remember to rest, to put down my phone, my keyboard, my pens, and just rest. Just still myself and practice being. My nondominant left arm reminds me to accept and love my weakness, my vulnerability, my limitations.

Both of these—being still and being loved—remain attitudes that I try to cultivate daily.

Which is easier in theory than practice.

Such as the day I had last week when the world seemed to be moving in slow motion while I rushed to keep appointments, return calls and texts, meet with staff, and check in on loved ones who were struggling. I sat on I-70 in Denver traffic twice as long as typically required to get to a doctor's appointment.

There, I checked in only to be told my doctor was running late because he had unexpectedly had to operate on a patient that morning. I counted seven other people sitting and staring at their phones throughout the waiting room. When I was finally taken back to an exam room, almost an hour had passed.

After rescheduling the rest of my afternoon, I needed to pick up the prescription my doc had called in to my pharmacy before heading back to my office. I pulled into CVS to find the drive-thru line indistinguishable from the full parking lot.

*Deep breath, Michael, deep breath. Hold it, count . . . and exhale.*

So I parked and went inside to stand in line along with a dozen others. Weary and defeated, I scanned the faces of the other customers. A casually dressed mom holding a sick toddler. An elderly couple in hiking apparel talking loudly in order to hear one another. A teen with more piercings than tats scrolling on her phone. A suited corporate executive losing his cool and demanding to speak to the manager.

An assortment of ages and stages who, like me, had to be there but didn't want to wait.

A smile began to take shape, and I took another deep breath before beginning to practice God's presence. I let go of the tension in my shoulders and neck, the tension of being ready for flight or fight. I surrendered to circumstances and asked God to meet me with an awareness of his peace and presence right where I stood, next to a display of canes and orthopedic braces. Which I realized I might need before I got out of there.

Part of me threw shade at my desire to connect with God, recalling that it had been a few days since I had read from the Scriptures or set aside time for intentional prayer and stillness. While I had half a dozen fresh and stimulating devotional books downloaded on my phone, I hadn't read from them all week either.

The more I thought about it, the more I realized that practicing the traditional spiritual disciplines I'd learned was sporadic at best. But they also tended to be a primary measure of my faithfulness and performance for God. So could I really expect to experience God in the midst of my overwhelming frustration when I hadn't been doing my part?

*Yes, I could.*

Half an hour later when I drove away, my mindset had shifted. I was no longer in a rush, having embraced that I didn't need to do all that I had scheduled. That being present to God in the moment was possible. That I had recognized that I had a choice about how I responded to the pileup of delays that had derailed my busy day. That spiritual practice is more about how you experience God throughout your day rather than checking off a to-do list of activities.

## TELL ME WHO TO BE, NOT WHAT TO DO

Spiritual mentors have always been an important part of my life. In my college years when my faith was growing, I craved the companionship of men and women who embodied the calmness, wisdom, compassion, and strength I longed to know for myself. I went into performance mode to impress these leaders, demonstrating my intelligence and humor, my earnest desire to know God and heal from my painful, chaotic childhood. Throughout college, I continued my apprenticeship to spiritual leaders who seemed to have the faith thing figured out.

Shortly after graduation, followed by meeting my wife and our marriage, I pursued learning from the Christian thinkers, teachers, authors, and counselors who resonated with my desire for more than a surface relationship with the divine. Reading their books, listening to their lectures, and attending their conferences led to moving across the country to Colorado in order to experience and learn a pastoral counseling model, including the opportunity to study with Dan Allender.

My time with them in that graduate program led to opportunities to meet and interview my spiritual fanboy all-star list: Eugene Peterson, Philip Yancey, Dallas Willard, Brennan Manning, Chaim Potok. While the depth and frequency of my relationship with these giants of the faith varied, I inevitably asked them the question that burned inside me: What do I need to do to grow in my faith? Can you tell me what's required to know God, emulate Jesus, and walk by the Spirit on a daily basis?

My mentors responded with kindness, curiosity, and thoughtful suggestions. Many reiterated the building blocks of faith that had become so familiar they were almost clichéd: a quiet time of daily prayer each morning, Bible study, reading devotional books, serving those in need around me, and participating actively in a local church. In almost every case, I was already practicing these disciplines, and they honestly didn't seem to be working. I wanted to drive a Lamborghini on a Le Mans course, not continue to pedal around the neighborhood with training wheels.

I believed that if I just knew what to do, or how to do what I was already doing differently and better, then my inside would align with my outside, closing the gap where I had often found myself freefalling. I would experience more peace and serenity, become more aware of God's presence and hear his voice clearly. The power of my addictions and compulsive behaviors would wane as I replaced their appeal with my desire to know and love God. There had to be a system, a skill set, a technique, a program, or a process that could deliver the spiritual substance that I considered the secret to life.

No matter how diligently I did the spiritual disciplines required to be a "good Christian," I still felt disappointed and eventually resentful. Either I was doing my part and God wasn't showing up to do his, or else I still had not cracked the code on what to do in order to experience him the way I longed to know him. To relate to him like the new mentors I was discovering, both ancient and modern pilgrims and sages whose dedication to what I had once dismissed as rote devotion to orthodox superstition now resonated with me.

They all knew something, had something, and therefore must do something that I wanted for myself. So throughout much of my adult life, I tilted toward extremes when it came to practicing my faith, oscillating between dutiful diligence that I assumed should be rewarded or angry resentment resulting in letting the practice of spiritual disciplines fall away.

Thankfully, I learned that I was asking the wrong question.

Instead of trying harder on what I should be doing, I discovered how to practice simply being.

## NOTHING IS EVERYTHING

Depending on your past experiences with spiritual disciplines or practices, you may have turned to this chapter first. That would have been what I would do if I picked up this book fifteen or twenty years ago. Or you may have been tempted to skip this chapter altogether, and you're just skimming this now to see where I'm going and what I could possibly have to say about practices that you haven't heard before. And depending on what you've heard and tried before, the answer may indeed be: *nothing*.

The difference, however, is that I hope your perspective has shifted just a little on what it means to experience God and live a life of faith that aligns with your beliefs. The trouble with spiritual practices is that they can become disciplined obligations inaccurately reflecting the status of our relationship with our Father. That's why, for starters, I prefer using the term practices rather than disciplines. Yes, self-discipline is utilized and exercised, but most of our associations with discipline lean toward discouragement, deprivation, and detachment.

Disciplines can sound like such habits are punitive or penitent, actions that must be taken to confirm that we're doing it right—"it" being our life of faith. Disciplines tempt us to infer that if we skip them, alter them, ignore them, discontinue them, well, then that means we're obviously *un*disciplined. And an undisciplined person lacks willpower and stamina, instead reflecting weakness and halfheartedness, immaturity and impulsiveness.

On average, doctors train for at least twelve years before they can practice medicine professionally. Then they continue practicing. Even after decades of gaining wisdom and experience, they're still said to be practicing. They know that practice is not merely science but perhaps more art. The collected sensibilities and gleaned insight never stop.

Spiritual practices are the same. They reflect the ongoing process of becoming awake and alive, an awareness that we are not pursuing perfection but wholeness. Becoming human. Embracing our humanity created in the image of God. Being intentional to explore and cultivate God's presence in our being and in our living.

They're less about doing anything and more about being present.

Practice only makes perfect when perfect means whole and integrated, present and securely attached to God. Practices keep us humble and allow for error, for distraction, for alteration, for busyness, for daily curveballs that upend our mood and mindset. We don't have to do them, and therefore we look forward to doing them as a means of closing the gap, inviting God into all the moments of our day—regardless of what we're doing.

Which brings us back to the other distinct aspect of spiritual practices: they're not about *doing* anything but about *being* present. There's a way of being spiritually present to all the things we experience during our day, which is the essence of practice, not just the ritualistic or religious habits and routines. Even doing nothing can be a practice, ironically enough, which reflects the biblical notion of Shabbat, ceasing action and resting in God's presence.

Practice is about showing up.

Being mindful of God when you wake up, when sipping your coffee, when driving the kids to school, heading to the office, enduring another video conference, meeting a friend for lunch, working out at the gym, shopping for groceries, cooking dinner, loading dishes and cleaning the kitchen table, folding laundry, flipping to the cool side of our pillow in the middle of the night. Author and speaker Barbara Taylor Brown agrees: "Hanging laundry on the line offers you the chance to fly prayer flags disguised as bath towels and underwear."

One of the best-known and most-beloved advocates for integrating spiritual practices into union with God's presence was the seventeenth-century French monk known as Brother Lawrence of the Resurrection, or simply Brother Lawrence. Serving as a lay brother in a Carmelite monastery in Paris—the same religious order as my aunt, Sister Ann—he was assigned to the kitchen to prepare food and cook for the other members of his order. During his time peeling potatoes, stirring soup, and washing pots and pans, Brother Lawrence attuned himself to God's presence with him.

Brother Lawrence wrote privately about this unique intimacy he enjoyed with God, and after the monk died, his writings were collected into the classic text of faith called *The Practice of the Presence of God*. In simple language, this unassuming monk makes it clear that it doesn't matter what you do; in order to experience God, it matters how aware you are of him while you're doing anything and everything. Brother Lawrence explained, "It is not necessary to have great things to do. I turn my little omelet in the pan for the love of God."

So basically, whatever we do provides an invitation to be grounded in the love of God's presence. Each new day provides fresh opportunities to practice the presence of the One within us and surrounding us. To join our mortal being with immortal love.

## WORKS WON'T WORK

If it doesn't matter what we do as much as being securely attached to God as we do it, then how do we sustain that divine connection? Simply put, by heeding Brother Lawrence—and many other saints and pilgrims through the centuries—and learning to focus our attention continually on the presence of love. I once heard Dallas Willard say that the first act of love is the giving of attention.

Consider how this truth is reflected in your interactions with your spouse, your children, your coworkers, your friends and family. If you're reading something on your phone and your spouse asks you a question, even a mundane or trivial one, you probably look up and gaze in their direction—and if you don't, you likely get called out on it at times. When our children were small, they would rush to greet me as soon as I walked through the door in the afternoon or evening. They couldn't wait to hug me, welcome me home, and tell me all about their day. Imagine if I had ignored them and acted indifferent, refusing to engage and receive what they offered. Not who I would want to be for them.

I also think of times when our young family would go to some friends' home for dinner. While the adults gathered in the kitchen or on the back deck to catch up, the kids would play in another room. Every so often, though, they would wander in and come to me or Julianne and grab our hand or lean into us. They wanted to touch base and know that we were still there. That everything was okay. That they could venture off to play while having a sense of safety and security.

Similarly, we show our love for others through gifts, time to-gether, all those ways that speak to their particular love languages. But we cannot make them love us by what we give and do. You can bring all the flowers, jewelry, and luxury items to your spouse or beloved, but those gifts will never convince them to love you. You cannot earn, merit, or manipulate yourself into a loving relationship with God—he already loves you.

I recall back in the early days of our marriage how I would often compensate and assuage my guilt for acting out with porn by cleaning the house before Julianne would return from errands. I'd feel so ashamed for wasting time and escaping into sexual fantasies that rather than face those feelings and the truth of my inner poverty and genuine need, I would distract myself by vacuuming, dusting, scrubbing, and organizing. Close to the time my wife would arrive home, I'd light a scented candle, put flowers in a vase on the table, pour her favorite beverage over ice, and place it along with a snack on the side table next to her comfy chair in our living room.

It might have worked a time or two, but Julianne caught on to my compensation attempts—I'm not exactly sure how—rather quickly. She would come home, greet me, and kick off her shoes. She would then share about her day and ask about mine while to-tally ignoring the obvious efforts I'd made. Her message seemed clear: "I'm not sure why you're doing these things, but I'm not impressed and won't be manipulated." I avoided risking anything vulnerable and tried to control her response to me. This doesn't work with God any more than it did with Julianne.

Vulnerability, the kind that opens us up to experience God, never demands or pressures, refuses to create expectations or to feel entitled. It is a posture of the heart that comes from a place of poverty and humility, of honest need and authentic desire. And vulnerability requires courage. Paul describes this as the key to receiving the free gift of grace and remaining securely attached to God's love, mercy, and goodness. "For it is by grace you have been saved, through faith—and this is not from yourselves, it is the gift of God—not by works, so that no one can boast" (Ephesians 2:8-9).

Remember, grace is opposed to earning, not to effort.

Relying on works to attain and sustain relationship leads to comparative assessment, about being good enough or not good enough. This is the analytical, quantifiable, legal way of understanding relationship, similar perhaps to the way a prenuptial agreement outlines the assets and division of property for a marriage relationship. But Paul emphasizes that this is not the way we attain our salvation because it relies solely on divine grace evidenced by God's love that we accept by faith. No one can do more or less than anyone else. We are all in need and have access to the love and grace of God.

So rather than hide our neediness and escape from our brokenness, we are free to steward them as currency in how we connect with God. Our surrendered heart learns to rest in the embrace of the Trinity.

Our brokenness becomes the doorway—not the dead end—for entering a new space where we commune with God, in union with him.

### KNIT IN THIS KNOT

Once you accept that knowing God is not about what you do or what you do the right way, you shift the way you relate to all that is holy. You notice the divine all around you. Because practicing your experience of God's presence begins with paying attention. With being awake to the present moment, not lost in ruminations on the past or projections into the future. With being here and now, wherever and whenever that is.

So take a deep breath right now and hold it for a few seconds before slowly releasing it through your mouth. What do you feel in your body as you breathe?

Consider all that is going on around you. What's your view right now? Familiar furniture and decor at home? Trees and sky beyond your park bench? What do you hear? The chatter and cutlery clanging in the café where you're reading this? The birdsong-to-silence of early morning as you scroll to the next page? And smells—car exhaust and diesel fumes from the nearby highway? Cinnamon rolls just out of your oven? How does the chair feel or the ground beneath your feet?

Let me say it again: *spiritual practice begins with paying attention.*

Another memorable saint coined the term *oneing* to describe our ongoing awareness, secure attachment, and spiritual union with God. Julian of Norwich, who lived during the Middle Ages, explains in *Revelations of Divine Love*:

> This beloved soul was preciously knitted to God in its making, but a knot so subtle and so mighty that it is oned in God. In this oneing, it is made endlessly holy. Furthermore, God wants us to know that all the souls which will be saved in heaven without end are knit in this knot, and oned in this oneing, and made holy in this holiness.

Oneing is becoming like a little child and running to God again and again. We talk to him, listen to him, still ourselves in his presence. We practice his presence and rest in his goodness. Oneing is knowing who we are, whose we are, and feeling the comfort, the peace, the purpose, the certainty of love's presence and promises. We are seen, soothed, safe, and secure in ways that more than fulfill us and fill the cracks and valleys in our parched and weary soul.

## ACTIVE STILLNESS

In addition to paying attention and oneing, practicing God's presence also requires understanding the tension between knowing what we are supposed to do and what God is supposed to do. Simply put, our part in this relationship is the beloved, the recipient and conduit of divine love, with this reception and reflection only possible when we open ourselves to experiencing God. God's part is to reveal who we know him to be in a personal, intimate, and supernatural relationship.

This kind of understanding also requires realizing that our role is active, not passive, and empowered by God's Spirit. Rather than work harder, try different techniques, or give up altogether, we can rest in stillness, bask in simply being with the One who loves us most. Julian observed, "The place which Jesus takes in our soul he will nevermore vacate, for in us is his home of homes, and it is the greatest delight for him to dwell there." Jesus confirmed to his followers, "And surely I am with you always, to the very end of the age" (Matthew 28:20).

Aware of our role as God's beloved, we discover that certain habits and actions facilitate our ongoing relationship and present experience of him. Daily practices can create space which allows us to enjoy all that love pours into us. One of the essential practices involves cultivating stillness and experiencing silence. This may sound counterintuitive, that an intentional practice is about being still and quiet, but it's an ancient idea emphasizing what we need to be more attuned to God.

We get to still the noise within and hear God's voice.

We learn to be present to ourselves so that we are able to be present with God.

We discover more of our authentic self so we can experience more of the God that looks like Jesus.

Practice and presence are related, then. As we practice being present with divine love, we also learn to be present with who we are and to be present with other people around us, accepting them as they are, where they are, just as God meets us.

Often when we're not actively practicing the presence of God, we're unable to be present to ourselves and feel overcome by our fear, anger, shame, sorrow, loneliness, anxiety, and depression. Connected and in union with God, however, we can accept and even welcome all parts of ourselves, even the ones we don't like or don't want. Everything belongs. No longer do we have to hide, run, fight, deceive, or manipulate ourselves and others.

When practicing the presence of God becomes our priority, we can pray with the psalmist: "One thing I ask from the LORD, this only do I seek: that I may dwell in the house of the LORD all the days of my life, to gaze on the beauty of the LORD and to seek him in his temple" (Psalm 27:4).

Securely attached to our endless source of love, we can rely on him, trust in him, and walk with him.

## ICARE PRACTICES

Sometimes when I think about spiritual practices and the challenges I experience, a favorite quote comes to mind, "Our present age constitutes a virtual conspiracy against the inner life." In other words, we must be intentional and consistent. We must make room for spiritual practice in all aspects of our being.

In order to facilitate and sustain our experience of union with God, we practice embodied spirituality, which integrates our body, mind, emotions, and will. This allows us to practice God's presence like Brother Lawrence and other saints and mystics who realized the immediate accessibility of their divine union no matter what they were doing during the day. As we have explored, being aware of our body and its sensations and needs allows us to be more aware of the divine, both in us and around us. This is why a regular somatic practice such as walking, hiking, swimming, or simply sitting in nature can reinforce our experience of God being with us, his love metabolized in our bodies. Aware of our human bodies, we allow each action and activity to be mindful, faithful, prayerful. Nothing is too mundane or insignificant.

We also implement practices that enhance our contemplation and union with God in ways that allow us to detach from the worldly busyness that wants to consume us. Many of the ancient habits include fasting—either from food or other substances, including social media, that distract us from our awareness of the divine—along with centering prayer, lectio divina, meditation, acts of service, and creativity. None are required or formulaic; they're simply options that provide different ways to connect and experience different aspects of God.

Finally, it's helpful to practice a way of being present to your self, one that helps you prepare to be present with God, a practice which facilitates your secure attachment to him. While there are innumerable ways to create and utilize such a practice, the one I've formed and recommend to those I counsel is called ICARE. I think of these five progressive elements as helping you create an intentional foundation so you can "do nothing" with God—in other words, just experience union with him and be present with yourself.

There's nothing particularly mystical or magical about the ICARE practices. For me, they simply help me practice the message of my tattoos—be still and be loved. Without this practice or similar reminders, I resist being still and overlook being loved.

Another benefit of practicing ICARE is simply learning to be aware and pay attention to your body and your inner world. Or as Curt Thompson likes to say, "Pay attention to what you pay attention to."

The ICARE practice also helps you connect to your center, to remain with yourself when overwhelmed by thoughts and feelings, to create space for yourself, to awaken and enliven to what is before you, already present.

Our images of God are not easily dislodged. Which is why these practices are transformational, not transactional. Because in God's economy there is no transaction. There is only love freely given. Every time we practice, we are allowing in and welcoming the reality that love has us. There's an old Celtic saying that you can't put the ocean in a thimble, but you can put a thimble in the ocean. Practices provide a way to put our thimble in the ocean of God's love.

### I = INQUIRE. "WHAT'S HERE RIGHT NOW?"

Focus on what's going on in the present moment, including all that you're sensing, feeling, and experiencing. For example, are you having racing thoughts, churning in your stomach, or tightness in your shoulders?

Inquiry allows you to recognize what's going on inside of you, in your body, mind, heart, and soul. Rather than shutting down when something painful, troubling, or unfamiliar comes up, you can face it and identify it. You can become a student of yourself in a way that makes more of an opening for God's presence and your experience of his love.

### C = CENTER. "BE HERE RIGHT NOW."

Focus on what you need. Notice what your body and emotions are telling you. Take a breath and drop down to your center.

Centering yourself means taking a step back, dropping down from the often layered or overwhelming assortment of thoughts, feelings, desires, impulses, and sensations you're experiencing. Centering means finding your physical, spiritual, and emotional reference point in your body. For many, this is in the center of their chest, somewhere near their heart. Here, you become present to the current moment by gaining awareness of your senses, the way you inhabit your body, the kinds of thoughts running through your mind, and the feelings emerging. Over time, you learn to center yourself in ways that provide a comfortable place of stillness in order to relax and reset. Centering keeps you from being swept away by an overwhelming tide of thoughts, feelings, and sensations or from shutting down because of them.

## A = ACCEPT WITHOUT JUDGMENT.
## "WELCOME WHAT'S HERE."

Focus on welcoming all that you're sensing and feeling, regardless of how uncomfortable or unpleasant it may seem.

Acceptance often prevents your default shame and judgment from kicking in, recognizing that everything in you is holy and welcome. You no longer have to run or hide, numb or escape. Securely connected to God, you can face the hard things, the unimaginable losses, the devastating injuries, the excruciating pain, and the unbearable shame.

## R = REMAIN. "STAY RIGHT HERE."

Focus on continuing to be present. You may calm yourself with your breathing as you remain in the present moment.

Remaining with yourself in the midst of disappointment, discomfort, and distress is not easy—that's why we find substances, experiences, and people who take us out of them. Yielding to the limitless presence of love allows you to stay with whatever you're experiencing. When love has you, you practice recognizing how this awareness can shift your perspective. You can receive the care you need in order to handle whatever is going on. You can humbly ask for help when needed and accept it without shame.

### E = EMPATHIZE. "BE KIND TO WHAT'S HERE."

Focus on keeping judgment, self-condemnation, and self-criticism suspended as you simply accept and attend to all you're experiencing with curiosity and kindness.

Empathizing with yourself and for yourself calls to mind the instruction we find in Colossians 3:12: "Therefore, as God's chosen people, holy and dearly loved, clothe yourselves with compassion, kindness, humility, gentleness and patience." Clothing yourself with this sense of kindness allows you to be just who you are and to cultivate compassion and acceptance. This biblical idea of self-compassion allows us to see ourselves lovingly, to soothe ourselves with kindness and gentleness, to cultivate safety with patience, and to securely rest in God's love.

Again, ICARE is not a magic formula or guaranteed steps to end your struggles or fix your problems. It is simply a process to use and practice in order to be present with yourself, to show compassion and kindness to yourself, and to reinforce the serenity of being God's beloved child. If you know or can create a different method that better suits your needs and current circumstances, please do so with my blessing.

Remember, the thing about practice is being, not doing.

It's about showing up.

Paradoxically, in order to do nothing and simply experience God, there are some ways to prepare, to step back from distractions, and to attune yourself. These spiritual practices—or "spiritual practicals" as one spiritual director I know likes to call them—contribute to the overall divine practice that's already available. Think of it as different channels, Julian's oneing, that all lead to One.

Grounded by love in you and around you, practice becomes the pleasure of his presence.

Your soul is restored as you continually embody your connection with God.

## BLESSING

*May you view practices as practical ways to experience
the fullness of love.
May you surrender using practices to earn favor
with God or merit his grace.
May your practices allow you to recognize how beauty
and suffering reveal God.
May your practices allow you to be present with yourself
so you can then be present with God.*

# 12

# OVERFLOW

OPENING OUR HEARTS TO VULNERABILITY

*No single raindrop ever considers itself responsible for the flood.*

KHALED HOSSEINI

In 1995 I had the joy of interviewing Eugene Peterson for the *Mars Hill Review*. As we sipped coffee just brewed from his French press, I asked Eugene to describe his biggest concern for believers in America. His answer didn't surprise me: "Christians are growing more spiritually thin and impoverished." I immediately felt the weight and truth of his words in my own life. Sitting in his apartment in Vancouver, I was there as a contributing editor for a journal, but I was literally delivering pizzas to earn income while in grad school. And still grappling with the fallout from blowing up my life and marriage.

Today the irony of Eugene's words is not lost when the smartphones in our pockets contain more Bible study resources than Martin Luther had throughout his entire life. But information can't change a human heart. More knowledge about God and the Bible won't produce life-giving experience with God.

For more than thirty years I've had a front-row seat to the glory and ruin that is Christianity in America. The privileged view from where I currently sit is my psychotherapy and spiritual direction chair, where I work almost exclusively with Christian leaders. From this vantage point I listen and watch and offer loving presence as they engage their story in all its joy and heartbreak.

Another vantage point I've had is from my professorial office, where I've trained seminary and graduate students for over thirty years. I've taught them to think deeply about life with God, personal transformation, and how God interacts with our process of change. My students have gone on to work as pastors, missionaries, mental health counselors, academics, and spiritual directors. The common theme most share today is having owned how their life story has shaped the person they've become. As we therapists like to say, "They've done their work." Which makes the rigors of graduate school look comparatively easy.

I see this professionally, but I can't escape that these are themes continuing to play out in my personal journey as well. Doing *my* work, and continuing to do my work, offers me the clearest vantage point of all. Because I live and teach and counsel and write as a broken man.

As I've shared with you, I've been on a journey to wholeness—even when it didn't look like wholeness—most of my life. At five years old I attended my first Alcoholics Anonymous meeting as my father arrived early to set up chairs and make coffee. At age nine I lived in a trailer park after moving across the country with my family to participate in drug rehab for my brother. At sixteen I was hospitalized for mental health issues. As a young married man I lived a double life and almost destroyed my marriage. And I continue to participate in twelve-step groups as I continue to recover what's been lost.

I've learned that my experiences, both the wonderful and the devastating, can lead me to experiencing God in ways that leave me spinning like the cabinet with the nuns. One moment I'm separated and disoriented, and the next I'm dancing around doing the hokey pokey.

You can experience the fullness of love and enjoy its abundance, but it requires deciding what—or Who—will hold you and how you want to live the rest of your life. It's not too late. You can become securely attached to God, even when you've lived up until now with insecure attachment.

You can continue being a raindrop but not part of the flood.

Or you can embrace being in an ocean of divine love.

Please understand it's not an all-or-nothing kind of binary choice—those only leave us widening the gap. Instead, it's an all-and-everything kind of choice.

The part of you that wants this and the part of you that doesn't are both welcome.

The part of you that can be faithful and the part of you that has been unfaithful.

The part of you that loves God and the part of you that doubts if he even exists.

The part of you that wants to surrender to gravity and the part stuck in the centrifugal force of your own efforts.

As you begin to reconsider and rebuild a new kind of faith, you can either focus on closing a faucet flowing with toxic water or opening a fountain overflowing with living water. Imagine one source with red, rust-flecked sludge trickling out of it that you must somehow stop. Now envision the other pouring out sun-sparkling clear water that splashes over you with the kind of cool, life-sustaining refreshment needed on a hot summer day.

On a bookshelf in my office, I have a piece of wood with two metal fixtures protruding—one is a spigot handle and the other is a flow-valve lever. Spigots attach to faucets and water sources to tap into them and provide access. Flow valves, however, control the source of water for entire homes, buildings, or city blocks.

I spent the early years following Jesus trying to screw down the spigot of sludge. Now I am trying to open the flow valve and drink, splash, and share clear, cool refreshment from the fountain of living water. Stop the sludge or drink living water.

So often in seeking more spiritual substance in my life, I worked hard to stop the faucet of toxic temptations, leaden shame, and sinful contamination. My thinking went something like this: if I can eliminate as much of the bad stuff as possible—the triggers and temptations, distractions and destructive detours—then I'll experience more of the good stuff, the joy and peace and purpose I longed to savor and share with others.

Yeah, it didn't work. No matter how many times I regrouped, found a new paradigm or thought leader, gained a fresh perspective on Scripture, or formed different habits, as long as my objective remained focused on stopping the flow of dirty, stagnant water, I remained thirsty. I sincerely wanted to know God and to be a blessing to other people with the gifts he's given me, but in this dirty-water-off mindset, I burned out quickly, spiritually dehydrated by deprivation of what I needed most.

I've seen so many others hit a wall from the same misguided strategy. They show up at the church and do as much as possible. They serve others, knowing there were once aspects that they enjoyed. But without fresh, living water to hydrate them and saturate their being, they dry up and burn out.

Eugene Peterson once told me that one of the enemy's greatest strategies is getting people into Bible study three times a week. If you've read this far, then you probably don't need to know more about the Bible. You need more personal experience of God. Instead of studying the written Word, you long to know the living Word Made Flesh who is the God that looks like Jesus.

## LOVE OVER LEGALISM

As I eventually realized the futility of this limited strategy, I shifted to considering my needs more than my flaws and weaknesses. I had been conditioned, of course, to view my needs as the source of most problems, all my needs lumped into the category of carnal desires rather than the legitimate, healthy, God-given needs required for living from love. But as my way of seeing myself and God and others changed, I started focusing on the goodness within me, within others, and throughout the world because of who God is, the source of unlimited, unconditional love. My needs seem sinful only when I keep trying to shut off the filthy-water faucet.

When I began to heal from trauma and grow my experience of attachment, only then could I experience that love has me. Healing from trauma grows our capacity for attachment. I began relating to God differently, no longer striving but discovering the practice of being, and the spiritual practices that facilitate oneing with God. I no longer considered my needs as dangerous or indulgent but as embodied indicators of the divine in me. Learning to trust that love has me has become the foundation of my life with God. It's how the gap has continued to close.

Obstacles still abound within us, though, because learning to live in union with love is a process, an ongoing journey of discovering what each new day, new relationship, new event, new opportunity reveals. Even though we know it's a process, an ambling divine road trip, we may start driving faster and forget to still ourselves. Even as you shift your vision and begin to see more with the eyes of your heart, you may revert to old ways of ceaseless striving or just giving in to your brokenness at times.

I'm reminded of an incident someone described to me involving an apparent conflict between a missionary teacher and an advocate for survivors of sex trafficking. These two women served within the same organization working to end human exploitation in various countries around the world. The advocate often helped young men and young women find jobs after they had spent a year healing and transitioning from their former trauma. So there was nothing unusual when she placed a young Romanian woman with the cleaning service utilized by their ministry organization's main offices there in Cambodia.

The young woman was a hard worker, and all went well until the missionary teacher discovered her using vodka to clean the whiteboards in the conference room. At first the teacher accused the cleaning lady of drinking alcohol on the job, but the young woman explained that it was next to impossible to get the alcohol-based cleaner needed to erase and clean the whiteboards, so she improvised with what was readily available and comparable—cheap vodka, which she kept stored in a file cabinet.

The teacher remained skeptical and decided to write a letter to the mission's board of directors about the inappropriate offense. Even if what the cleaning woman had said was true, the teacher assumed they would be just as alarmed as she was to know that vodka was stored on the premises of their overseas offices. Surely alcohol had no place in ministry, regardless of how it was supposedly being used.

The advocate for survivors intercepted the teacher's letter and responded like Jesus did with the moneychangers in the temple. Keep in mind this woman had seen the worst horrors possible with human trafficking—children younger than ten forced into prostitution by their families, pimps in urban areas using physical violence to control their captives, gang leaders who got kids hooked on drugs before they were sold for sex. So in light of the urgent work of their mission to rescue and liberate these young lives while eradicating the variables that make trafficking possible, this advocate was outraged.

They were trying to save lives, restore health to the weak and defenseless, reunite families, and stop international criminals, and her colleague was worried about half a bottle of Smirnoff stashed in a file drawer? A bottle that was actually an ingenious hack used by a resourceful woman intent on doing her job despite lacking what she needed. Her panoramic perspective reflected God's priorities more than the propriety of appearances.

So often, things are not as they seem. Like the missions teacher, we're looking for God's official whiteboard cleaner and refuse to consider what he might provide to do the job. We're scandalized because there's vodka stashed in a file cabinet and miss seeing the desperate, urgent needs of other humans around us.

I share this story because it reminds us how we revert to legalistically having to get it right when we're not daily surrendering to love, willing to be anchored by love. The timeless good news, though, is that even when we try to live by legalism rather than love, God remains in love with us, literally. He has never stopped loving us and never will.

## HERE I AM

Welcoming our brokenness tends to keep our eyes open to love and dispel the old cataracts that want to cloud our vision. We realize that secure attachment to love provides everything we need to live and love from a place of wholeness and fullness. And when we forget, or lose sight of his love because of distractions and diversions, God always gets our attention and reminds us that we're not alone, that he is present with us, always eager to experience our union with him.

During those momentary lapses when I lose my way, I now take comfort knowing I'm not really lost. In the depths of my addictions and struggles, I sometimes despaired and wondered if I could ever experience God the way I longed to know him, if I could ever experience healing and wholeness and the *more* I had always hungered to find. In those moments I felt like a small child, one who's wandered away from his parents in a large crowd.

You've likely experienced this scary separation yourself, either when you were a child or as an adult with the children in your care. I recall being at the mall with my son, CJ, when he was a toddler of three or four. We ran into a friend, another dad there with his kids, who were both a couple years older than CJ. While the kids played, the dad and I caught up and talked about our families, our work. After about ten minutes, we reached a natural stopping point and went in our separate directions.

Only CJ was nowhere to be found.

Neither my friend nor I had noticed him disappear. I assumed my son was playing with the others. But my friend's two kids hadn't seen where he went either. Adrenaline spiked my heart rate as if my son had been kidnapped by traffickers. In light of my own story, my mind went blank. Overwhelming emotions—panic, guilt, fear, anger—flooded my body.

We all began searching, going up and down the mall, the food court, into and out of each store. CJ was nowhere to be found. After about ten minutes of searching, I was about to find mall security when I heard my friend's daughter yell, "Found him! Here he is." She took my hand and led me back into a toy store specializing in collectibles and remote-controlled cars. Lying on his stomach on the carpeted floor at the end of an aisle was my son, playing with cars on a Hot Wheels track.

He was unfazed by our separation and smiled up at me. "Hi, Daddy!" he said, as if I had been the one who had wandered away from him. "Hi, Bud!" I said and brushed away my tears, bending to join him on the floor, eager to be close to him.

He was safe and secure, and so was I.

I recently read about a similar situation occurring in Argentina. A young boy named Juan Cruz became separated from his father, Eduardo, in a crowded outdoor plaza in Buenos Aires. But father and son were quickly reunited because of the well-known custom practiced by many South American cultures. As soon as they begin walking, children are taught what to do if they're away from home and become separated from their mom, dad, grandparent, or caretaker. They're told to find the nearest adult, tell them they've lost their person and need help finding them.

What happens next is simply beautiful.

The adult then picks up the child and lifts him onto their shoulders. They begin shouting "Lost! Lost!" along with the child's name. This results in immediate applause from everyone around them. They continue clapping and chanting the child's name until they attract the parent's attention to come forward and reunite with their lost child. There's a brief video online of Juan Cruz's experience, along with similar reunions in Brazil and other nearby places.

As I consider Edwardo and the tradition of lost children, I think of my own story. I picture myself separated from the security of the ones I love. I don't know how to get back. I picture myself in that barroom basement, far from the security of those who should have protected me. I don't know how to be okay. Only later would I risk telling someone that I'm lost. To let them lift me up, speak my name, come around me, and chant in unison. Over time I have been securely rejoined to lost parts of myself and more deeply connected to God and others.

This is why the cabinet when I was four years old remains such a powerful metaphor.

Because when the doors open after spinning and being disoriented, we discover love has us.

## LOVE EXTRAVAGANTLY

It's a no brainer: human beings want to love with abandon, generously and extravagantly. If you're awake and alive, you want to love from deep inside. But love cannot be internalized until it is metabolized.

When our bodies metabolize food or sugar, alcohol or medication, we ingest and then digest. We take it in, and it becomes part of us, fueling us, sustaining us, healing us. We metabolize love when we allow it to fill us, again and again, cleansing our wounds, washing away our pain and sorrow, quenching our deepest thirsts, saturating us with the Spirit.

God's love works the same way within us, within our bodies and within our very being.

The vision of restoration begins with God's kindness with us, but it extends to our participation in the restoration of all things.

Brokenness clears space for us to experience more of God if we're willing.

There is an imperishable seed inside us. When we pull away the rubble of our flaws and failures, our addictions and compulsions, our disappointments and dissatisfaction, we find there is still love. We experience restoration in community, nurturing the imperishable love inside us. The seed planted for eternity begins to sprout and grow and push up through the rubble. Just as a blade of grass or a dandelion can crack open a concrete porch or asphalt driveway, love growing in us has the power to crack and shatter the layers of our past vulnerability.

As this disruption takes place, we discover stillness and solitude becomes the place where new life begins to grow and flourish. You may not see it or feel it or even believe it, but the reality remains the same: *love has you.*

The apostle Paul, rendered by Eugene Peterson, explains it so well:

We don't yet see things clearly. We're squinting in a fog, peering through a mist. But it won't be long before the weather clears and the sun shines bright! We'll see it all then, see it all as clearly as God sees us, knowing him directly just as he knows us! But for right now, until that completeness, we have three things to do to lead us toward that consummation: Trust steadily in God, hope unswervingly, love extravagantly. And the best of the three is love. (1 Corinthians 13:12-13 MSG)

Love has you and will continue to overflow—in your heart, your life, your relationships, your work, your play, in all facets of your life. Love transforms you from the inside out so that as you experience wholeness and healing, divine love spills out of your brokenness for others to experience. You can then share with them the living water of love and the One who is its eternal source.

As we reach the end of our shared connection on these pages together, I hope that you find yourself just a little more open, a little more at ease, a little more centered. You may not believe a word I've written, or you may feel like your beliefs have been clarified and your heart radically transformed.

Either way, my prayer for you remains the same:

### BLESSING

*May you see where you are and always know*
*the love of God.*
*May you experience the abiding joy of union with God.*
*May your vulnerability and availability to love change*
*the world.*
*May you always know that love has you.*
*Forever and ever. Amen.*

# ACKNOWLEDGMENTS

My deepest thanks to the many friends and family who inspired, encouraged, supported, reviewed, or otherwise loved this book into existence.

Dudley Delffs, thank you for giving editorial shape and substance to my vision and doing it with such skill, wisdom, and friendship. And deep gratitude to everyone at InterVarsity Press— thank you to Cindy Bunch for such a warm welcome to the IVP family, to Rachel O'Connor for being so attentive with the details, and to Lori Neff and Krista Clayton creatively sharing the book with the world. And very special thanks to my literary agent, Kathy Helmers, whose generous heart is matched only by her expert wisdom and passionate advocacy.

To my clinical colleagues at Restoring the Soul: Julianne Cusick, Brian Boecker, Janelle Hallman, Ben Wilson, Renee George, and Cindy Marrone. Thank you for allowing me to share my ideas, and for offering such grace to this quirky dude. I'm so proud to serve together with you. To those who have helped lead and direct Restoring the Soul: Clint and Shelly Morse, Clint and Heather Johnson, Dave Lowe, Jake Smith, Peter Zaremba, and Dan Schwartz. To the RTS Weekend Intensive staff who always give me permission and encouragement to improvise and grow the concepts throughout this book in real time. Thank you.

To my spiritual parents, caregivers, and directors: thank you to Jeff Coakwell, Joel LaRiccia, Father Roger Bower, and Father

John Lager. To Curt Thompson, Jim Smith, and Brad Jersak—thank you for your friendship and for supporting me spiritually and intellectually with your books and ideas. To Ian Cron and Peter Zaremba for a lifetime of deep friendship.

And to those who have significantly influenced and blessed me through their work and writing: Jorge Mario Bergoglio, Richard Rohr, Ronald Rolheiser, Thomas Keating, Martin Laird, James Finley, David Benner, J. Phillip Newell, Dallas Willard, Daniel Ladinsky, Wendy Farley, Dr. Barbara Peacock, Dan Siegel, Bessel van der Kolk, Sue Johnson, Frank Anderson, Richard Schwartz, Iain McGilchrist, Gabor Maté, Andre Dubus, Regis Martin, and Heather King.

To the artists whose imaginations have helped restore me to sanity: Mako Fujimura for showing me the beauty of kintsugi; Marc Chagall for creating beauty from horror; Bruce Springsteen, Bono, Bruce Cockburn, and Rob Mathes for getting me from there to here with twelve notes and twenty-six letters. To Chaim Potok and Khaled Hosseini, who always give shape to my turmoil. Admiration and gratitude to the three women of old whose work and lives have nurtured and nourished my soul and imagination: Julian of Norwich, Teresa of Ávila, Thérèse of Lisieux.

To my sisters Colleen, Barb, and Kate, for filling in the gaps then and now with love. And to Sister Anne Cusick, for the life and love you gave so freely from behind that serpentine wall. To my children—CJ and Lily. And finally, to Julianne with love—you are my person.

Love has each and every one of us.

# GUIDE FOR LEADING
# A GROUP

Participating in a group studying almost anything can be awkward and challenging.

Participating in a group exploring the gap between what you believe and what you experience—downright terrifying. But one of the most powerful ways to discover more about what you believe and no longer believe, about how to securely attach to God in a way you've never experienced, about what you want to experience spiritually and what you want to move beyond is to participate in a community of like-minded individuals. Wrestling with faith, with the discontent and disappointment of past Christian experiences, can leave you feeling isolated and alone. But joining a group discussion of this book can be a safe and productive way to process and apply the ideas you want to consider with other sojourners.

It might be helpful to have a group discussion leader but not essential. The key is for each participant to engage with other group members as you discuss your thoughts in response to the questions provided for each chapter. The focus is not on right answers (there are none) or getting through all the questions. The focus is on being present with one another and listening with your ears as well as your hearts.

You will want to nail down the following elements in order for your group discussions to go as well as possible:

**Format:** Will you meet online or in person? Who will send out the e-vite or arrive early to set up the physical space?

**Location:** Depending on the format selected, where will you meet? Homes, churches, classrooms, community centers, and outdoors (weather permitting) are all good options.

**Time:** After polling participants, set a time to begin and decide how long you want each of the six discussion sessions to last. Begin on time and end on time unless everyone agrees to allow the discussion to end naturally.

**Respect:** Everyone should participate and be welcomed into the group conversation. Crosstalk and talking over others should be discouraged. Try to listen attentively when others speak, knowing you will have plenty of time to share your own thoughts.

**Confidentiality:** Affirm at the beginning of each discussion session that your group conversation will remain confidential among group members, unless someone specifically requests and receives permission to share outside the group for a valid reason.

**Compassion:** Focus on how you can listen and help one another move forward as you think about your personal faith, what you believe, and how you want to live out what you believe. Enjoy the discourse as a rich way of not only enhancing your reading experience but of growing spiritually as well.

# QUESTIONS FOR REFLECTION AND DISCUSSION

## SESSION 1

1. Spinning: Escaping and Experiencing God's Embrace

   - The beginning of this chapter recounts a memory that has become a metaphor for Michael's spiritual journey. What detail or phrase jumped out as you read this passage? Can you think of a significant memory from your childhood that reflects the evolution of your faith?

   - Michael writes, "For the last thirty years, the straightforward yet complex question shaping my life and work has remained more or less constant: How do human beings grow spiritually, emotionally, and psychologically? Basically, I want to know if people can change—if I can change—without compromising the deepest, truest part of ourselves." Based on your life experiences, what are some of the key events—positive and negative—that have caused you to grow spiritually, emotionally, and psychologically?

   - Do you believe you can experience profound spiritual change while remaining true to yourself? Why or why not? Explain your answer.

   - What has been the greatest hindrance or obstacle as you have pursued a relationship with God? When have you tried to grow closer to God only to find yourself farther away?

2. Delta: Closing the Gap Between Believing and Knowing

- How have you experienced the gap between what you wanted to believe about God and what you knew from the reality of life? How has this gap influenced your journey of faith?

- Which experiences in your life have eroded your faith over time? In other words, what are the moments and memories that cause you to distrust God and experience distance?

- On a scale of 1 to 10, with 1 being "terribly disappointed" and 10 being "incredibly fulfilled," how would you rate your level of satisfaction with your personal faith journey as you have experienced it? Explain your score.

- What does it mean for you to shift from striving in your faith to experiencing "unforced rhythms of grace"? What must change in order to complete this shift?

**SESSION 2**

3. Attached: Being Held and Beheld

- Do you agree with the basic premise of attachment science, that our experiences with our caregivers from infancy to young adulthood establish our patterns of relational response?

- When applying attachment science to your own childhood and upbringing, what stands out to you? Which of the Four Ss—seen, soothed, safe, and secure—was most lacking in your early development?

- Our attachment style (the degree to which we've been seen, soothed, safe, secure) not only shapes our human relationships; it also determines how we experience being seen, soothed, safe, and secure with God.

  Do your attachment style and childhood experience reinforce this hypothesis? Or do you struggle to affirm it? Explain your response.

- How are you currently attempting to experience what you should have received but didn't from your parents or primary caregivers? Think about what you do to force others to see you, the ways you self-soothe, or what it takes for you to feel safe and secure with others.

4. Evil: Rejecting the Lies About God and About Ourselves
   - Do you agree with Michael's statement, "Evil is one of those concepts that we inevitably identify from a distance—torture, abuse, suffering, genocide, mass murder, terrorist attacks, war crimes—but struggle to see how it plays out in our own lives"? How would you define evil based on your own observations and experiences?
   - What are some of the lies that evil has attempted to sow in your life? What falsehoods have you accepted and experienced harm from believing?
   - How have the two essential lies sustaining evil—that God is not good and that you can be God—tried to take root in your life? How have these two lies fueled your addictive behavior and pain-management choices?
   - What are some of the most important truths for you to remember in order to refute old lies and false assumptions of the past? What is true about who you really are? About who God is?

### SESSION 3

5. Embodied: Connecting to Our Bodies and Connecting to God
   - Like the example of Geoffrey at the beginning of this chapter, how have you experienced physical dissonance between your faith beliefs and your life experience? How did this disconnect manifest in your body?

- The body is the context in which the spirit operates. We cannot separate spirit and emotions. God is certainly both. Created in his image, our spirit operates within our human body. With the incarnation of Jesus, God fully experienced living in the form of his human creation. The solution for our spiritual struggles then emerges where they all intersect: . . . *Embodiment.*

    How have past faith experiences and belief practices influenced you to separate the spiritual and physical realities of your life? What impact did this have on you and your view of God?

- When has your body served as a "truth teller" for what was actually going on inside you? What are the physical symptoms and sensations your body uses to try and get your attention when there's a disconnect between your spirit and your body?

- How has your physical body allowed you to experience God in a sensory way most recently? How can paying attention to your body's messages draw you closer to God?

6. Turning: Discovering We Are Broken, but Not Bad

- What's your response to Michael's description of hitting rock bottom in an adult bookstore only for it to become the conduit of encountering the grace of Jesus? When have you been able to identify a glimmer of redemption in one of your lowest or most painful moments?

- Which of the 5 *W*s—wretchedness, weakness, woundedness, wiring, and warfare—have you typically used to explain your mistakes and moral failures? Why has that particular *W* seemed to be the cause of your struggles?

- Personalize the following statement to reflect a new perspective on how you struggle:

_____ is sinful . . . and results

from _____

_____

_____.

- Reconsider what you just wrote and imagine Jesus being with you right now and saying, "Of course, of course, you struggle with this." What rises up in you as you hear him say this?

## SESSION 4

7. Wholly: Becoming Whole and Holy

- How has your view of God's holiness kept you at a distance from knowing him more personally and intimately? What's the basis for your view of God's holiness?

- As I see it, holiness is all about wholeness and best viewed by reflecting on our humanity. It's about a new way of living and relating to God anchored by the reality that we are seen, soothed, safe, and secure. Holiness invites us to live in union with the God who looks like Jesus.

  What stands in the way or impedes your willingness to shift your understanding of holiness? How would your faith change if you shifted to this new definition of holiness? Why?

- Do you believe that God the Father loves you as much as he loves Jesus? What stands in the way of accepting that this is true?

- God restores us into something more and better than before. We become his handiwork, his *poiēma*, his workmanship, his kintsugi. God's holiness, like the precious gold and silver in kintsugi, unites our broken pieces into a new wholeness. So rather than suppressing, hiding, condemning, shaming, and numbing the parts of our stories we don't like or want to include, we discover how they become raw material for a new creation.

How is God currently reshaping the broken pieces of your life into his new creation? Where do you see evidence of the way God's holiness is bringing you into a new wholeness?

8. Known: Facing Our Deepest Desire and Greatest Fear

- What's an example of how your hide-and-seek way of being known by others manifests in your life? What are you willing to let others know about you in order to withhold something more shameful?

- "In a thousand different ways, shame whispers and shouts that being known and loved is dangerous and impossible." When has shame recently tried to impede your willingness to be vulnerably known? What are the lies that shame uses to prevent you from being known?

- When we are not known, when we believe the lie that love does not have us, then we die inside. Until we face that loss that feels like death, we cannot be fully reborn in the resurrection power we find in knowing Christ.

  What truths have you resisted facing about yourself and your life? What defense systems or self-protective behavior have you used to keep these truths unacknowledged?

- When have you experienced being vulnerably known and still accepted by another person? What was the context for this experience? What did you risk in order to be known so authentically?

**SESSION 5**

9. Mysticism: Experiencing Spiritual Oneness with God

- Which of the three methods for knowing God—your senses, your intellect, your spirit—has become your default way of experiencing his presence and communicating with him? Which of these three methods requires you to take risks outside your comfort zone?

- What are some of the ways you have attempted to experience God and "know the unknowable"? Which moments remain memorable because of the intimate connection you experienced with God?

- Review the Mystical Considerations that Michael lists near the end of chapter nine. Which one of these resonates with your own experience the most? Why? What other mystical considerations would you add to this list?

- Have you ever considered yourself a mystic before reading this book? Would you consider yourself one now, based on how Michael defines and describes it? Why or why not?

10. Imagination: Learning to See with the Eyes of the Heart

- Do you believe an active imagination is essential for pursuing relationship with God? How has your imagination enhanced your journey of faith?

- In order to reconstruct our faith, to close the gap between our beliefs and our experience, the imagination must be reclaimed and relied on as the ignition of our mystical experience of God.

  What's required for you to reclaim you imagination and rely on it to ignite a more intimate experience of God? What are the false assumptions and misguided beliefs about the imagination that must be dispelled?

- Do you agree that "the imagination is fueled most powerfully by beauty and suffering"? Why or why not? How have both beauty and suffering shaped your imagination and therefore your view of God?

- What are the works of art (literature, music, film, sculpture, painting, etc.) that have consistently engaged your imagination? Which places and natural locales repeatedly allow you to experience God more fully?

### SESSION 6

11. Practice: Embodying Our Connection with God

- I believed that if I just knew what to do, or how to do what I was already doing differently and better, then my inside would align with my outside, closing the gap where I had often found myself freefalling. . . . There had to be a system, a skill set, a technique, a program, or a process that could deliver the spiritual substance that I considered the secret to life.

  When have you held a similar belief and pursued knowing God through a new system, practice, program, or process? What did you learn from that experience—about yourself? about God?

- Considering your past experiences, would you make a distinction between spiritual disciplines and spiritual practices? If so, what's the difference? What's one spiritual habit that consistently draws you closer to God's presence?

- When have you tried to compensate for your shortcomings and earn God's favor through your actions, service, or generosity? How have those experiences shaped the way you continue to relate to God?

- What stands out to you about developing a self-care practice such as ICARE? Which of the five components—Inquire, Center, Accept, Remain, Empathize—seems most challenging to you? Why?

12. Overflow: Opening Our Hearts to Vulnerability

- When I began to heal from trauma and grow my experience of attachment, only then could I experience that love has me. . . . I began relating to God differently, no longer striving but discovering the practice of being, and the spiritual practices that facilitate oneing with God. I no longer considered my needs as dangerous or indulgent but as embodied indicators of the divine in me. Learning to trust that love has me has become the foundation of my life with God. It's how the gap has continued to close.

  Do you currently tend to view your needs as dangerous and indulgent? Or as indicators of the divine getting your body's attention? Explain your answer.

- Reread the excerpt above. What's required for you to continue closing the gap between what you believe and what you experience? Why?

- When was the last time you felt alone and bereft in the midst of a painful struggle, powerful addiction, or traumatic response? How can you experience God even when going through these times when you feel apart from him?

- What has surprised you most as you've read this book and experienced its message? What shifts or changes are taking place in the way you live out your faith as a result?

# NOTES

## 2. DELTA

18  *Martin Laird has explained*: Martin Laird, *Into the Silent Land: A Guide to the Practice of Contemplation* (London: Darton, Longman & Todd, 2006), 12.

## 3. ATTACHED

21  *The work of Dr. Curt Thompson*: Curt Thompson, *The Soul of Desire* (Downers Grove, IL: InterVarsity Press, 2021), 31.

23  *Thompson explains, "Security is . . . "*: Thompson, *The Soul of Desire*, 32.

24  *Our survival strategies*: To explore this connection between addiction and attachment, you should read Gabor Maté, MD, *In the Realm of Hungry Ghosts: Close Encounters with Addiction* (Berkeley, CA: North Atlantic Books, 2010).

25  *John Bowlby's research*: "What Is Attachment Theory?" The Attachment Project, www.attachmentproject.com/attachment-theory.

26  *Attachment refers to*: Curt Thompson, *The Soul of Shame* (Downers Grove, IL: InterVarsity Press, 2015), 52.

28  *Our attachment style*: For an in-depth exploration of this idea, read Krispin Mayfield, *Attached to God* (Grand Rapids, MI: Zondervan, 2022).

## 4. EVIL

41  *Bradshaw's description of addiction*: John Bradshaw, *Healing the Shame That Binds You*, expanded and updated ed. (Deerfield Beach, IL: Health Communications, 2005).

45  *Geneen Roth confirms*: Geneen Roth, *When Food Is Love: Exploring the Relationship Between Eating and Intimacy* (New York: Penguin, 1992), 18.

    *"Eye of the Hurricane"*: David Patrick Wilcox, "Eye of the Hurricane," by David Patrick Wilcox, *The Alarm*, Universal Music Publishing Group, 1987.

## 5. EMBODIED

55   *"Hebrew good"*: "God's Goodness Is Dynamic," May 1, 2023, The Center for Action and Contemplation, https://cac.org/daily-meditations/gods-goodness-is-dynamic-05-01/.

56   *The ways trauma manifests*: Bessel van der Kolk, *The Body Keeps the Score* (New York: Penguin, 2015), 12.

60   *"Most . . . have a heavy burden"*: Thomas Keating, *Invitation to Love* (New York: Bloomsbury, 2012), 110.

## 6. TURNING

67   *Thérèse of Lisieux considered*: Thérèse of Lisieux, *Story of the Soul: The Autobiography of St. Thérèse of Lisieux*, 3rd ed., trans. John Clarke, OCD (Washington, DC: ICS Publications, 1996).

71   *unless pain is transformed*: Richard Rohr, *The Wisdom Pattern: Order, Disorder, Reorder* (Cincinnati, OH: Franciscan Media, 2020).

74   *"Our attachment patterns"*: Curt Thompson, *Anatomy of the Soul: Surprising Connections Between Neuroscience and Spiritual Practices That Can Transform Your Life and Relationships* (Carol Stream, IL: Tyndale Refresh, 2010).

77   *"You bent down over"*: Fr. Roger J. Landry, "The Mercy That Can Make Even Our Sins Happy Faults, Easter Vigil, March 26, 2016," *Catholic Preaching*, March 26, 2016, https://catholicpreaching.com/wp/the-mercy-that-can-make-even-our-sins-happy-faults-easter-vigil-march-26-2016/.

## 7. WHOLLY

88   *"Every time you make a choice"*: C. S. Lewis, *Mere Christianity* (San Francisco: HarperOne, 2023), 12.

## 8. KNOWN

102   *"When we feel certain"*: Bob MacArthur, *sacredlead*, "A Light . . . to Someone Somewhere," September 5, 2021, https://sacredlead.com/2021/09/05/a-light-to-someone-somewhere.

## 9. MYSTICISM

112   *God's hiddenness*: Ronald Rolheiser, "The Hiddenness of God and the Darkness of Faith," RONROLHEISER, OMI, November 30, 2015, https://ronrolheiser.com/the-hiddenness-of-god-and-the-darkness-of-faith.

114   *Rolheiser's reflective explanations*: Rolheiser, "The Hiddenness of God."

## 10. IMAGINATION

125 *"Two hemispheres of my mind"*: C. S. Lewis, *Surprised by Joy* (New York: Harcourt Brace Jovanovich, 1955), 170.

127 *Need "a way of looking"*: Iain McGilchrist, *The Master and His Emissary: The Divided Brain and the Making of the Western World*, 2nd ed. (New Haven: Yale University Press, 2019), 24.

    *Most . . . rely on one*: McGilchrist, *The Master and His Emissary*, 27.

128 *Simone Weil noted*: Simone Weil, *Simone Weil: An Anthology*, ed. Siân Miles (New York: Grove Press, 2000).

131 *Coleridge and Wordsworth using the arts:* Malcolm Guite, *Lifting the Veil: Imagination and the Kingdom of God* (London: Canterbury Press, 2021).

## 11. PRACTICE

140 *"Hanging laundry"*: Barbara Taylor Brown, *An Altar in the World* (San Francisco: HarperOne, 2010), 74.

141 *"I turn my little omelet"*: Brother Lawrence, *The Practice of the Presence of God* (New Kensington, PA: Whitaker House, 1982), 16.

143 *Grace is opposed to earning*: Dallas Willard, *The Great Omission: Reclaiming Jesus's Essential Teachings on Discipleship* (San Francisco, CA: HarperOne, 2014), 34.

144 *"This beloved soul"*: Julian of Norwich, quoted in "Oneing," The Center for Action and Contemplation, May 12, 2020, https://cac.org/daily-meditations/oneing-2020-05-12/.

145 *"The place which Jesus takes"*: Julian of Norwich, quoted in "Oneing," Center for Action and Contemplation.

146 *"Our present age"*: Jan Walgrave, quoted in Ronald Rolheiser, *Forgotten Among the Lilies: Learning to Love Beyond Our Fears* (New York: Image/Random House, 2007), 18.

## 12. OVERFLOW

160 *Lost child in Argentina*: Sara Barnes, "This Is How a Crowd in Argentina Reunited a Lost Boy with His Dad," *My Modern Met*, August 30, 2022, https://mymodernmet.com/lost-child-argentina.

# FURTHER READING

*Anatomy of the Soul: Surprising Connections Between Neuroscience and Spiritual Practices That Can Transform Your Life and Relationships* by Curt Thompson, MD (Carol Stream, IL: Tyndale Refresh, 2010).

*Attached to God: A Practical Guide to Deeper Spiritual Experience* by Krispin Mayfield (Grand Rapids, MI: Zondervan, 2022).

*The Body Keeps the Score: Brain, Mind, and Body in the Healing of Trauma* by Bessel van der Kolk, MD (New York: Penguin, 2014).

*The Connected Life: The Art and Science of Relational Spirituality* by Todd W. Hall (Downers Grove, IL: InterVarsity Press, 2022).

*Embracing the Body: Finding God in Our Flesh and Bone* by Tara M. Owens (Downers Grove, IL: InterVarsity Press, 2015).

*Forty Days to a Closer Walk with God: The Practice of Centering Prayer* by J. David Muyskens (Nashville, TN: The Upper Room, 2007).

*The Gift of Being Yourself: The Sacred Call to Self-Discovery* by David G. Benner (Downers Grove, IL: InterVarsity Press, 2015).

*In the Realm of Hungry Ghosts: Close Encounters with Addiction* by Gabor Maté, MD (Berkeley, CA: North Atlantic Books, 2010).

*Into the Silent Land: A Guide to the Christian Practice of Contemplation* by Martin Laird (Oxford, UK: Oxford University Press, 2006).

*Open Heart, Open Mind*, 20th anniv. ed., by Thomas Keating (London: Bloomsbury Continuum, 2023).

*The Soul of Desire: Discovering the Neuroscience of Longing, Beauty and Community* by Curt Thompson, MD (Downers Grove, IL: InterVarsity Press, 2021).

*Surrender to Love: Discovering the Heart of Christian Spirituality* by David G. Benner (Downers Grove, IL: InterVarsity Press, 2015).

*Try Softer: A Fresh Approach to Move Us out of Anxiety, Stress, and Survival Mode— and into a Life of Connection and Joy* by Aundi Kolber (Carol Stream, IL: Tyndale Refresh, 2020)

## BECOMING OUR TRUE SELVES

The nautilus is one of the sea's oldest creatures. Beginning with a tight center, its remarkable growth pattern can be seen in the ever-enlarging chambers that spiral outward. The nautilus in the IVP Formatio logo symbolizes deep inward work of spiritual formation that begins rooted in our souls and then opens to the world as we experience spiritual transformation. The shell takes on a stunning pearlized appearance as it ages and forms in much the same way as the souls of those who devote themselves to spiritual practice. Formatio books draw on the ancient wisdom of the saints and the early church as well as the rich resources of Scripture, applying tradition to the needs of contemporary life and practice.

Within each of us is a longing to be in God's presence. Formatio books call us into our deepest desires and help us to become our true selves in the light of God's grace.

### LIKE THIS BOOK?

*Scan the code to discover more content like this!*

*Get on IVP's email list to receive special offers, exclusive book news, and thoughtful content from your favorite authors on topics you care about.*

IVPRESS.COM/BOOK-QR